CRITICAL RACE ENGLISH EDUCATION

Johnson's visionary and much-needed book is a call for the transformation of English education to embrace rather than reject Blackness. Confronting the context of heightened racial violence against Black youth that continues to sweep across the United States, Johnson illuminates the interconnection between the physical and symbolic violence that unfolds in and outside the classroom and demonstrates the harm this causes to Black youth. Employing an original framework, Critical Race English Education, Johnson reveals how English education and ELA classrooms are dominated by eurocentric language and literacy practices, and provides a justice-oriented framework that combats anti-Black racism. Throughout the book, Johnson disperses love letters to Blackness, Black culture, and Black people, which serve as actions and practices for positive thinking and self-awareness about Blackness. Critical Race English Education is a movement for Black lives.

A crucial resource for pre-service ELA teachers, researchers, professors, and graduate students in language and literacy education, and sociology of education, this book offers classroom lessons, thematic units, sample activities, and other pedagogical and curricula practices that reconceptualize ELA pedagogies in humanizing ways and cater to the needs of students who come from racially and linguistically diverse backgrounds.

Lamar L. Johnson is Associate Professor of Language and Literacy for Linguistic and Racial Diversity in the Department of English at Michigan State University, USA.

NCTE-Routledge Research Series
Series Editors: Valerie Kinloch and Susi Long

Alsup
Teacher Identity Discourses: Negotiating Personal and Professional Spaces

Banks
Race, Rhetoric, and Technology: Searching for Higher Ground

Daniell/Mortensen
Women and Literacy: Local and Global Inquiries for a New Century

Rickford/Sweetland/Rickford/ Grano
African American, Creole and other Vernacular Englishes in Education: A Bibliographic Resource

Guerra
Language, Culture, Identity, and Citizenship in College Classrooms and Communities

Haddix
Cultivating Racial and Linguistic Diversity in Literacy Teacher Education: Teachers Like Me

Brooks
Transforming Literacy Education for Long-Term English Learners: Recognizing Brilliance in the Undervalued

Baker-Bell
Linguistic Justice: Black Language, Literacy, Identity, and Pedagogy

Nash, Polson, Glover
Toward Culturally Sustaining Teaching: Early Childhood Educators Honor Children with Practices for Equity and Change

Bryan
Toward a BlackBoyCrit Pedagogy: Black Boys, Male Teachers, and Early Childhood Classroom Practices

Johnson
Critical Race English Education: New Visions, New Possibilities

The NCTE-Routledge Research Series, copublished by the National Council of Teachers of English and Routledge, focuses on literacy studies in P-12 classroom and related contexts. Volumes in this series are invited publications or publications submitted in response to a call for manuscripts. They are primarily authored or co-authored works which are theoretically significant and broadly relevant to the P-12 literacy community. The series may also include occasional landmark compendiums of research.

The scope of the series includes qualitative and quantitative methodologies; a range of perspectives and approaches (e.g., sociocultural, cognitive, feminist, linguistic, pedagogical, critical, historical, anthropological); and research on diverse populations, contexts (e.g., classrooms, school systems, families, communities), and forms of literacy (e.g., print, electronic, popular media).

CRITICAL RACE ENGLISH EDUCATION

New Visions, New Possibilities

Lamar L. Johnson

Taylor & Francis Group

NEW YORK AND LONDON

First published 2022
by Routledge
605 Third Avenue, New York, NY 10158

and by Routledge
2 Park Square, Milton Park, Abingdon, Oxon, OX14 4RN

Routledge is an imprint of the Taylor & Francis Group, an informa business

© 2022 Taylor & Francis

Library of Congress Cataloging-in-Publication Data
A catalog record for this title has been requested

ISBN: 9780367276430 (hbk)
ISBN: 9780367276423 (pbk)
ISBN: 9780429297052 (ebk)

DOI: 10.4324/9780429297052

Typeset in Bembo
by Deanta Global Publishing Services, Chennai, India

CONTENTS

Acknowledgments   *vii*

Series Editors' Foreword   *ix*

*Foreword: Critical Race English Education: A Loving, Unapologetic
Critique and Trajectory for English Education*   *xii*

Introduction: A Critical Race Autopsy on Black Lives   1

LOVE LETTER I: MY DAD SAID I LOVE YOU ... AND I SAID IT BACK   **13**

1 But It Is about Race... "That's a Fact. Say It Louder for the
People in the Back"   17

2 The *Other* Trayvon: Anti-Black Racism and Violence against
Black Lives   34

3 Black(ness) Is, Black(ness) Ain't: Critical Race English
Education   49

LOVE LETTER II: MICHAEL BROWN AKA "BIG MIKE"   **65**

4 Doin' It Wrong: Rethinking Reading and Writing Workshop   69

5 Part I: "We Have to Bring It Real Hard, Who Else Gon' Give It to 'em?": Critical Race English Education and Humanizing Research through a Critical Family Book Club   86

6 Part II: The Elephant Is *ALWAYS* in the Room   106

LOVE LETTER III: PROMISED LAND   **127**

7 B(l)ack to the Future: Black Rage, Radical Love, and the Radical Imagination   129

Outro: A Story about Black Laughter and a Call for Spiritual Literacies   135

Afterword: Fearlessness and Insurgency in the Building of Black Fugitive Futures   *141*
Index   *143*

ACKNOWLEDGMENTS

Writing this book has been a beautiful and challenging experience. Even in my darkest hour, I never stopped writing. The encouragement, support, and care I received from my ancestors, family, and friends sustained me spiritually, mentally, and emotionally; and, my cup continues to overflow with an abundance of gratitude, love, and joy. To show my love and appreciation for those who supported me on this journey, I have utilized music and songs as a medium to illustrate my acknowledgments. In her dynamic book, *We Want to Do More Than Survive: Abolitionist Teaching and the Pursuit of Educational Freedom*, Bettina Love uses an array of songs across different genres of music to acknowledge those who supported her on her book journey. Building from the creativity and structure from Bettina, I have selected hip-hop, R&B, and gospel songs to share my love for those who helped me to bring this book project to fruition.

"Zion" by Lauryn Hill and "Just Kickin It" by Xscape—mom, Barbara Howard
"Rapper's Delight" by the Sugarhill Gang—dad, Robert Howard
"It's So Hard" by Big Pun—dad, Wade Lamar Brannon
"What a Wonderful World"—maternal grandmother, Fannie Johnson
"I'll Take You There" by the Staple Singers—paternal grandmother, Geraldine Christie
"Count on Me" by Whitney Houston and CeCe Winans and "I Like It" by Cardi B—Lesha Howard
"It Don't Have to Change" by John Legend—to my family aunts and uncles
"All We Got" by Chance the Rapper and "LA" by Ty Dolla $ign—Rob Elam
"Keep the Family Close" by Drake—cousins
"Schoolin' Life" by Beyoncé—Raymond Gordon
"Power and Mood 4 Eva" by Beyoncé—Dr. April Baker-Bell

"No Problem" by Chance the Rapper—Demetrius Cofield

"Holy" by Jamila Woods—Dr. Courtney Mauldin

"Get Me Bodied" by Beyoncé—Shel Lessington

"Exhale" by Whitney Houston and "Ella's Song: We Who Believe in Freedom Cannot Rest" by Sweet Honey in the Rock—Dr. Gloria Boutte *AKA Mama G*

"What about Your Friends" by TLC—Khadijah Abdullah, Dr. Jen Doyle, Stephanie Boutte, and Dr. Dywanna Smith, Shannon Schoultz

"No New Friends" by DJ Khaled—Zae Holland, Que, Ryan King, Jaelen King, Garridon Hankins, Aldric Morton, Jube, Patrick Ratliff, Anthony Chung, and Anthony Harris

"Universe" by Ty Dolla $ign—my LA family: Rachel Gordon, Valarie Armstrong, Corey Dashaun, Alex Sadaú, Aftin McKnight, Yony, and Canada

"B Ok" by Wiz Khalifa—Ken Johnson and Jonathan Boutte

"Crown" by Chika—former high school students

"We Got Love" by Teyana Taylor—the students and families from my research project

"Melodies from Heaven" by Kirk Franklin—Pleasant Grove Baptist Church

SERIES EDITORS' FOREWORD

What does it mean to love the hell out of Blackness, especially when we live in a world that misreads our Blackness, misrepresents our Blackness, and paints a negative image of our Blackness? … Critical Race English Education is a call for radical love in ELA classrooms, language and literacy studies, and English education. This radical love for Blackness and for Black life must run through the heart of teachers' curricular decisions and pedagogical practices.

— Lamar L. Johnson

As series editors, we welcome you into Lamar Johnson's work to center pro-Blackness in the English language arts (ELA) classroom. From a foundation that insists on the need for radical love of Blackness not only in secondary classrooms but also in language and literacy research and English education in general, and through important critiques of the centering of whiteness in existing practices (reading/writing workshop, for example), Johnson lays out reasons why and possibilities for a much-needed shift in thinking as educators and researchers move from esoteric discussions to real actions day to day.

Johnson's research-based and justice-driven representation of why and how educators must take a critical pro-Black stand is communicated through his conceptualization of Critical Race English Education. Originally introduced in his 2018 article in *Research in the Teaching of English*, this book's exploration of Critical Race English Education allows educators to delve deeply into ideologies and practices around their role in the fight against anti-Black racism. In the early chapters, Johnson provides an important model for educators as he shares his own histories, leading to his recognition that countering anti-Blackness through education is a necessary act of "resistance, self-determination, [and] being justice-minded." Interweaving critical autobiographical narratives and his experiences as a son, friend, mentee, mentor, student, and teacher, along with his descriptions of the surveillance and victimization of Black students in and out of schools, Johnson guides readers to recognize the impact of practices that ignore, misrepresent, and/ or decenter Blackness. In further chapters, Johnson takes us into important critiques of current ELA models asking and answering questions such as:

> What if the reading and writing workshop model decentered whiteness and explored the complex intersections of race, racism, whiteness, language, literacy and education? What if Black lives mattered in ELA classrooms when we workshop the canon? What if the reading and writing workshop model centered Black youth lived histories and experiences to shape teachers' perceptions, curriculum choices, and pedagogical practices?

The book is uniquely organized around three love letters which are, as Johnson writes, "expressions of love to Blackness, Black culture, and Black people." The letters bring us into Johnson's thoughts as he writes to his father, to Michael Brown, and to nurturers who are his ancestors and elders. These letters ground and connect all other elements of the book in ways that anchor an ideology of Blackness as love, a foundational tenet to Critical Race English Education. Thus, at the heart of the book is the need for revolutionary change that centers Black joy, history, resilience, and resistance as acts of love. We opened this foreword with Johnson's primary question: "What does it mean to love the hell out of Blackness, especially when we live in a world that misreads our Blackness, misrepresents our Blackness, and paints a negative image of our Blackness?" He answers this question by outlining Critical Race English Education as that which:

a. Challenges anti-Black racism, whiteness, white supremacy, patriarchy, and violence that unfold in school contexts and outside-of-class spaces.
b. Examines the historical and present-day relationship between literacy, language, race, and education by expanding the concept of literacies to include activist contexts and social movements.
c. Aims to work against dominant and canonical texts that exclude the knowledge of Black people and the racial and ethnic experiences of Black people across the Diaspora.
d. Stands on the Black literacies that Black people have created over time and continue to form. Black literacies work against anti-Blackness because these literacies illustrate an unconditional love for Blackness and Black people.

Like the other books in the NCTE-Routledge Research Series, this book takes a critical look at classroom practices as it speaks to both teachers and researchers and the ways in which research and practice must attend to the lives of people of color within and beyond P–12 classrooms. Important to our goals for the series, Johnson does not dictate a pedagogical formula for critical race teaching in the ELA classroom. Instead, he supports educators' exploration of *why* Critical Race English Education is necessary, laying the groundwork for teachers, teacher educators, administrators, and policymakers *to envision, design, and enact* pedagogical transformation in their own spaces. Also, while the stories in this book are drawn primarily from secondary school experiences, they are every bit as applicable across age levels from children's earliest years through and beyond graduate education.

Critical Race English Education: New Visions, New Possibilities joins our series of books that includes foci on equity, justice, and antiracist education; critical qualitative, quantitative, and mixed methodologies; a range of cutting-edge perspectives and approaches (e.g., sociocultural, cognitive, feminist, linguistic, pedagogical, critical, historical, anthropological); and research on the literacies of minoritized peoples as well as on diverse contexts (e.g., classrooms, school systems, families, communities) and forms of literacy (e.g., print, electronic, popular media). We hope you are moved to action in your own educational settings as you consider Lamar Johnson's conceptualization of a Critical Race English Education as a pedagogical "movement for Black lives." We are proud that his text joins other books in the series that have been carefully selected for their commitment to the role of educators in moving us toward a more equitable society.

Valerie Kinloch
Renée and Richard Goldman Dean and Professor of Education
University of Pittsburgh
USA
and
Susi Long
Professor, Instruction and Teacher Education
University of South Carolina, Columbia
USA

Reference

Johnson, L. L. (2018). Where do we go from here?: Toward a critical race English education. *Research in the Teaching of English, 53*(2), 102–124.

FOREWORD

Critical Race English Education: A Loving, Unapologetic Critique and Trajectory for English Education

Gloria Boutte

This book is at once a searing, loving, unapologetic critique of English education as we currently know it. It is also an invitation for transformation of the
field. The fact that Lamar offers this timely analysis indicates that he is invested
in wanting to see English education become more relevant and equitable for all
students. Indeed, fighting against oppression in classrooms and curricula is an act
of love for humanity (Freire, 1970/1999; Johnson, Bryan, & Boutte, 2019).

Against the backdrop of endemic oppression in schools and society—and in
this case in English language arts (ELA) classrooms—learning to include, love,
and respect all of humanity is both revolutionary and healing. Borrowing from
Derrick Bell's concept of *sober hope*, revolutionary love is related to *sober* love.
When I say that Lamar's conception of Critical Race English Education is an act
of love, I am using *sober love* as opposed to naïve or sloganized notions of super-
ficial love. Using a metaphor, naïve love can be thought of as being *drunk* with
love—being inebriated and not seeing clearly. When we are sober, we see things
for what they are. This means that Lamar understands that challenges are a part of
the process of transforming English education. I am certain he knows that push-
back and resistance may very well be a part of the process for transformation for
English education. Yet, he has held steadfast to the responsibilities that accompany
sober and revolutionary love and insists that Critical Race English Education will:
(1) reject attacks on Black humanity; (2) require honesty and candor in delibera-
tions about the sociopolitics of ELA curricula and instruction (*naming and dismantling the "elephant in the room"*); (3) necessitate telling, listening, and hearing the
stories of Black people and other minoritized cultural groups; and (4) serve as a
way to begin healing ourselves and future generations from the embedded racism
in ELA curricula and instruction.

The intensity of Lamar's writing in this transformational volume conveys how the impact of persistent and pervasive invisibility and distortions of Blackness in English language arts classes *has kindled his ambition to contribute to the transformation of English Education.* Lamar performs a metaphorical autopsy of English language arts content in K–20 classrooms and curricula to examine the degree to which Black content and perspectives are missing. Even when Black students cannot name or voice the insult regarding the absence of Blackness as part of humanity in classrooms, they are aware of it on a tacit level and are damaged by ongoing linguistic, symbolic, physical, systemic, and curricula/instructional violence. In fact, the parts of my textual lineage that were most liberating and influenced me the most happened *outside* of school. This lineage included books about cultures around the world that I voraciously read in fifth grade and checked out from the public library *on my own initiative.* This instilled in me a desire to travel around the world beyond my small town and to be intrigued by the seemingly endless ways of being *human.* Likewise, my leisure, but motivated, reading of the classic novel, *Roots,* by Alex Haley (1965) when I was in tenth grade and the reading of the *Autobiography of Malcolm X* resonated with me so deeply that it ignited or awakened a sense of anger about racism and inspired me to fight against racism—ultimately through my teaching, service, and scholarship as a scholar activist.

I would be remiss if I did not mention the *True Confession* magazines that I read as a teen that taught me about passion in life and troubles and relationships, albeit, sensationalized and white-focused. Sexual relationships were topics adults did not discuss with teens, but these were issues that my friends and I were very interested learning about. Other central parts of my textual lineage as a youth which contributed to the person who I am today are Black magazines like *Right On, Jet,* and *Ebony*—and, later, *Essence.* These magazines were mainstays in the lives of Black people and we eagerly read (and re-read) them because the topics were about us. Since half of my life as a youth was spent in the segregated south, I also had the benefit of having Black music, Black teachers, Black communities, Black churches, and Black love as the backdrop of my life. These *healing* comforts served as buffers that many youth in the "integrated" 21st century do not have.

At the risk of over-romanticizing my youth, I will also note that we eagerly watched Blaxploitation movies like *Superfly* because (I think) we were so desperate to see ourselves on the big screen that we did not realize the power of negative depictions and their effects. At the same time, these movies and television shows taught us our first lessons about criticality when we reflected on the messages. Yet I, like most K–12 students, still wanted to learn the content that school deemed important and wanted to ingest all of it so I could be considered to be smart according to the assimilationist definitions in school. Lamar, while troubled by the nagging respect for Blackness, was also one who survived the warfare of schooling for Black students. Too many Black students, though, do not survive, and too many white students learn schools as experts in white supremacy—much to the dismay of humanity.

The reason why this book, *Critical Race English Education: New Visions, New Possibilities*, is so valuable is that school curricula and content have changed little in the more than four decades since I finished high school. The intensity of emotions and thoughts conveyed in this book echoes mine in many ways, which is not surprising since Lamar is one of my "legacies." I am justifiably angry about the continuous exclusion and minimalization of Black thought, perspectives, and content in ELA—and other subjects as well. Of course, communities and families should and will continue to provide rich Black literary texts like the ones I had for our children. But it is important that schools do also—not only for Black youth but for all youth. Currently, white students are the beneficiaries in ELA classrooms. As Lamar explains, this has a positive compounding effect for them as well as a debilitating effect on students of color—particularly Black students as I explain later. This is why Lamar is not asking for permission to change ELA curricula and instruction, he is demanding it—on behalf of the millions of students who are enduring harm, albeit below the radar of most educators and students.

The concept of an *autopsy* is appropriate because all too often ELA curricula are filled with the stories and ruminations of dead, white men with an occasional sprinkling of the perspectives of people of color, women, LGBTQ, or other groups that are minoritized. Too often people of color are only presented in assimilationist ways—if at all. The whiteness ingested by Black students in ELA classes is undoubtedly 100 percent fatal to the spirits and souls of too many Black students—and to their physical bodies by default of the white and assimilated people of color who also ingested this white *poison* and who end up being in positions that allow them to have power over Black bodies. If we autopsied the Black bodies slain by police around the nation, we would undoubtedly fine large traces of negative messages of themselves that were consumed in schools. Even when antidotes of Black love were available to the people who were murdered (e.g., Trayvon Martin and Sandra Bland), an autopsy would have likely revealed that it was insufficient to overcome the hatred of Blackness that is so endemic in schools and society.

Lamar questions the role of ELA educators in the ongoing struggle for justice. Critical Race English Education requires reimagining language and literacy education and classrooms as sites of racial justice that work against myopic curricula and instruction to which Black youth are continuously subjected. He explains the narcissism and violence of whiteness in ELA classrooms and in schools which invades, eradicates, and displaces other realities. This pervasive whiteness laced with occasional Blaxploitative tropes has gone unnamed, unmarked, unchecked for too long (Morrison, 1992). Readers may detect also deep pain from Lamar as he explains the hurt associated with the cumulative effect of having one's reality omitted and/or distorted in K–20 instruction, curriculum, and policies and how this trauma is also reflected in society.

It should be clear why English education makes sense as a site of transformation. Like other subjects, whiteness in ELA courses is omnipresent and endemic.

Unlike other subjects, it is *mandated* for 12 years in K–12 schools—and more if one happens to attend college. It is the *official* language of the US. Even the focus on "Standardized" English is limiting and excludes African American Language, Mexican American English, Indigenous Languages, and other variations of English—not to mention other languages. As Joyce King and Hassimi Maiga (2018) noted, racism is embedded in the English language and Blackness takes on many negative connotations (e.g., black eye; to *blacken*; blacklist). In comparison to African languages such as Songhoy-senni where Blackness is extremely positive (e.g., Black sun—when the sun is at its fullest expression at noon; *hari bibi* [Black water]—clean water). Indeed, all languages have dual purposes—they are both a means of communication and a carrier of culture (Wa Thiong'o, 1981). English *transports* white culture.

Notably, Lamar intentionally uses what some may consider to be a non-conventional style of writing in some parts of the book. I applaud this as the tools of Blackness are essential in dismantling whiteness. In some ways, his writing is reminiscent of the documentary *Black Is, Black Ain't* that he mentioned in the book. In this documentary, Marlon Riggs and Nicole Atkinson (1995) use gumbo as metaphor for the rich diversity among Black people and explore the complexities of Black culture using song, interviews, historical clips, and a variety of other media. I often show this video in my majority-white education courses *Black is, black ain't—told thru aspects of Black culture.* I have had white students say, "I did not understand it," without any thought that Black and students of color often think the same thing about the whitified (Kinloch, 2007) curriculum and instruction that people of color are subjected to on a daily basis. This leads me to the larger question which Lamar intimates in the first chapter, *why is loving Blackness a precondition of appreciation for humanity?* Here I offer a prelude for what the reader will receive in this book.

If we can love Blackness—that which has been historically and currently intentionally positioned as the antithesis of whiteness—we have overcome what is arguably the largest "white" man-created hurdle in the world. That is, whiteness has been misinterpreted to be synonymous with humanity and superiority. Discursively then, if one can love that which has been despised and held in contempt (Blackness) (Dubois, 1903) and considered at the "bottom of the well" (Bell, 1992), then surely it is easy to love any other group of people who have not been subjected to centuries of symbolic and physical violence and disparagement. For me, learning to love ourselves as Black people is the greatest love of all and is intentional political resistance to anti-Black hegemony which denies the beauty and wisdom of Black people (hooks, 2006).

Critical Race English Education insists that Blackness must be loved in its own right—not oppositionally to whiteness. How can we learn to love Blackness? How can we learn to harness the power and beauty of Blackness?

While we understand intersectionality and convolution of Blackness with whiteness (Morrison, 1992) and the many social identities (e.g., gender, age, socioeconomic status) that we (Black people) have, the Blackness element, if extracted, is most compelling, sweet, provocative, beautiful, and political—if we allow it to be. The reason that loving Blackness is a precondition for loving humanity is that, because of the way social equations that operate are configured, every cultural group is measured by how close or far away it is from Blackness. If we can love the extreme, surely we can love the middle. While I am certainly not comparing degrees of discrimination among various groups, it is difficult for me to imagine any other group of people that has been persecuted so thoroughly, broadly, and long as Black people.

So I end with Lamar's first mediation: *We must love Blackness as a precondition to humanity*. Only then can we begin to transform ELA classrooms. This does not mean *excluding other groups*, but until Black people are free, neither will anyone else be free.

References

Bell, D. (1992). *Faces at the bottom of the well. The permanence of racism*. New York, NY: Basic Books.

DuBois, W. E. B. (1903). *The souls of Black folk*. New York, NY: First Vintage Books/The Library of America Edition.

Freire, P. (1970/1999). *Pedagogy of the oppressed*. New York, NY: Continuum.

Haley, A. (1965). *The autobiography of Malcolm X*. New York, NY: Random House.

hooks, b. (2006). *Black looks: Race and representation*. Brooklyn, NY: South End Press.

Johnson, L. L., Bryan, N., & Boutte, G. (2019). Show us the love: Revolutionary teaching in (un)critical times. *The Urban Review, 51*(1), 46–64. doi:10.1007/s11256-018-0488-3

King, J. E., & Maiga, H. O. (2018). Teaching African language for historical consciousness. Recovering group memory and identity. In J. E. King & E. E. Swartz (Eds.), *Heritage knowledge in the curriculum. Retrieving and African episteme* (pp. 56–78). New York, NY: Routledge.

Kinloch, V. (2007). "The White-ification of the Hood": Power, Politics, and Youth Performing Narratives of Community. *Language Arts, 85*(1), 61–68.

Morrison, T. (1992). *Playing in the dark. Whiteness and the literary imagination*. New York, NY: Vintage.

Riggs, M., & Atkinson, N. (Co-Producers). (1995). *Black is, Black ain't* [DVD]. Retrieved from California Newsreel http://newsreel.org/video/BLACK-IS-BLACK-AINT (87 minutes runtime).

Wa Thiong'o, N. (1981). *Decolonizing the mind*. London, UK: James Currey.

INTRODUCTION

A Critical Race Autopsy on Black Lives

Meditation #1
We must love Blackness as a precondition to humanity.

What if the field of English education and language and literacy studies were to perform a critical race autopsy on Black lives? What would these autopsies report? A critical race autopsy allows us to take a keen and thorough look at Black lives—it allows us to pick apart the historical and contemporary racial and gendered oppression against Black children, women, non-binary individuals, and men. This notion of a critical race autopsy builds from critical race theory (CRT), which demands that we thoroughly examine the endemic nature of race, racism, whiteness, and white supremacy (Bell, 1992; Ladson-Billings & Tate, 1995; Matias, 2016). In addition to CRT, I also build upon the notion of performing a historical autopsy (Kelley, 2016). In fact, Kelley explains that a historical autopsy illustrates how the anatomy of modern-day state violence is tethered to the enslavement of Black people, colonialism, white supremacy, patriarchy, and racial capitalism. The humanity and freedom of Black people have always been viewed as things that can be bought and sold. The displacement and racial violence against Black lives are prime examples of how Black people's bodies and lives are oftentimes commodified and seen as property.

If we were to perform a critical race autopsy on Michael Brown's body, the report would tell us that before Brown was physically killed by four bullets to the arm and two bullets to the head, that he was spiritually murdered by the hands of a system that criminalizes and dehumanizes Black boys and men. The report would tell us that Michael Brown was killed by an "armed agent of the settler state who was allowed to take his life for refusing to comply with the order to walk on the sidewalk" (Kelley, 2016, 17:17). The white male police officer was given the

DOI: 10.4324/9780429297052-101

permission to destroy Brown's body and that is evident because he was not held accountable (Richardson & Ragland, 2018).

Additionally, if we were to perform a critical race autopsy on Sandra Bland's body, the report would tell us that this country has an intimate history with the maltreatment of Black women (e.g., sexual harassment, rape, reproductive health issues, and human trafficking just to name a few). The critical race autopsy would report that "Black women and girls experience gendered racism, subordination, and criminalization in American institutions by various types of violence (discursive and physical) by state-sanctioned and naturalized systems and policies that go unquestioned and unchallenged" (Richardson & Ragland, 2018, p. 46). The killing of Black girls and women at the hands of state-sanctioned violence is situated in the troubled and intimate history of anti-Black racism and sexism against the bodies and lives of Black girls and women.

Critical race autopsies are intersectional, and they show how some Black people (women, trans, disabled, and economically disadvantaged individuals) are often erased from the movement for Black lives and racial justice. If we were to perform a critical race autopsy on Tony McDade's body, the report would tell us that this country has a history with marginalizing, oppressing, and criminalizing transgender individuals. The report would tell us that anti-transgender violence largely impacts the lives of Black and Latinx transgender and gender nonconforming people.

Performing a Critical Race Autopsy on the Life of the Living

It is important to note that this autopsy is metaphorical—in a sense, not only does this critical race autopsy take up the body of the dead, but it also takes up the life of the living. Although we typically do not conduct autopsies on living bodies, in light of anti-Black racism and whiteness, it is necessary that I use this critical race autopsy metaphor to consider what dehumanization looks like in English language arts (ELA) classrooms, particularly for our Black children and youth who are being spiritually murdered on a daily basis. The blood of Trayvon Martin, Jordan Davis, Michael Brown, Renisha McBride, Rekia Boyd, Aiyana Stanley-Jones, George Floyd, Breonna Taylor, Tony McDade, Walter Wallace Jr., Nina Pop, and Monika Diamond (we must say their names) has been spilled in the streets of the United States and inside ELA classrooms. While Black children and youth are dying at the hands of police and civilians, inside classrooms they are also dying spiritually at the hands of many teachers. According to Love (2017), when Black students are taught from a curriculum that stifles their experiences, voice, and knowledge, they experience spirit-murder. Spirit-murder is the psychological and emotional death Black youth experience from living in a world that embraces anti-Black racism (see also Williams, 1987).

The anatomy of modern classrooms serves as a space of anti-Black racism and non-being for Black people. What would the critical race autopsy report look like for the seven-year-old Black girl who was sent home from school because her hair was in locks? If we were to perform a critical race autopsy on the 11-year-old Black girl from New Mexico who was slammed to the ground for taking an extra milk from the school cafeteria, then what would the critical race autopsy illustrate? Thus, the spirit-murder of Black youth warrants that we engage in a critical race autopsy of Black lives. In our current racial climate, Black youth are subjected to physical violence and other forms of anti-Black racism and racial violence in school spaces.

The omission of critical race conversations is an example of racial violence. For example, the whitewashed, state-sanctioned curriculum and texts that Black youth are required to study misrepresent many aspects of their lived experiences. Oftentimes, when people hear the phrase *state-sanctioned violence*, depictions of police officers and police brutality come to mind (Maynard, 2017). However, state-sanctioned violence can also take shape outside of the criminal (in)justice system and can include institutions such as schools, hospitals, social services, child welfare, and immigration. When I say state-sanctioned curriculum, I am referring to the curriculum that derives from state and government-funded polices, practices, and procedures that police, surveil, and punish Black lives through the curriculum we teach. The state-sanctioned curriculum exercises violence and has historical and contemporary roots in the reproduction of anti-Black racism through perpetuating a curriculum that is rooted in white supremacist patriarchal control. The state-sanctioned curriculum represents a society that has an interest in all things that reflect white people, white culture, and whiteness.

Educators often view conversations around anti-Blackness, racism, and white supremacy as taboo topics that have no correlation to ELA, language, writing, or literacy, particularly because ELA classrooms are contested spaces that are dominated by white, monolingual, middle-class perspectives that lack criticality and racial consciousness. white literacy and language practices found in high school English curricula are antithetical to the Black literacies and language practices that Black youth bring into English language arts classrooms (Johnson et al., 2017; Richardson & Ragland, 2018). From my personal experiences, I have encountered teachers who have a deep admiration for a eurocentric and school-sanctioned literary canon that does not include the voices, experiences, and knowledge of people who look, move, and exist in the world like me.

Critical Race English Education Is a Movement for Black Lives

This book illuminates the heightened increase in the racial violence against Black youth that continues to sweep across the country. Concomitant with the historical (mis)treatment of Black lives, the racial violence directed at Black people in the US and abroad has both heightened and led this country to a new historical insurgence known as the #BlackLivesMatter movement. In this light,

#BlackLivesMatter hones in on the human aspect of mattering by rejecting dehumanization and anti-Black racism. I utilize the #BlackLivesMatter movement as a data reference point for analysis. I demonstrate the interconnection between the physical and symbolic violence that unfolds for Black youth within outside-of-school spaces (e.g., churches, neighborhoods, parks, playgrounds, gas stations, etc.) and the physical and symbolic violence that erupts inside PreK–12 classrooms (e.g., high suspension and expulsion rates for Black youth, overrepresentation in special education courses, underrepresentation in gifted education courses, the hidden curriculum, and the spirit-murder).

In *Critical Race English Education: New Visions, New Possibilities*, I examine how English education and ELA classrooms are dominated by eurocentric language and literacy practices and ideologies. I understand such practices and ideologies as acts of violence that constantly remind Black children and youth that their lives, language, culture, race, ethnicity, and humanity do not matter. #BlackLivesMatter is not inseparable from the educational inequities that intentionally marginalize Black youth—from systemic policies that limit and deny Black youth educational resources (Anderson, 1988; King, 2005; Foster, 1998), to the lack of culturally relevant and sustaining language and literacy practices (Boutte, 2015; Ladson-Billings, 2014; Paris, 2012), and the over-surveillance and punishment of Black bodies through inequitable policies and procedures (Dumas & Ross, 2016; Kirkland, 2013; Winn, 2013). #BlackLivesMatter compels educators to consider the mattering of Black lives within educational contexts. More specifically, #BlackLivesMatter compels the field of English education to ponder the mattering of Black lives within ELA classrooms. In this book, then, I aim to counteract the racial violence that erupts in ELA classrooms and in language and literacy studies by providing educators with humanizing practices that reject anti-Black racism ideologies pertaining to Black life.

Throughout this book, I draw on the concept of Critical Race English Education, which I introduced in an article published in the National Council of Teachers of English journal, *Research in the Teaching of English* (Johnson, 2018). In the article, I used the acronym CREE. Since that time, I have critically examined my own naming process, reflecting on the reality that, while I tried to provide a simplified version of Critical Race English Education, the word CREE represents proud peoples who have also been historically and are currently oppressed by white dominant policies and practices. Since my conceptualization of Critical Race English Education is inclusive of Indigenous Peoples of North America but also focuses broadly on all peoples of color with a primary emphasis on anti-Black racism, in this book, I decided to not use the acronym. Instead, I discuss my conceptualization of the need for racial criticality in secondary education for exactly what it is: Critical Race English Education. Critical Race English Education is a movement for Black lives. The development and praxis of Critical Race English Education derive from deep within—it's undergirded in Black rage, radical love, and the radical imagination.

Purposefully, I center the self to better illustrate the various knowledges that contribute to my conceptualization of Critical Race English Education as a developing theory and framework. Boutte (2015) reminds me that theory is derived from our personal experiences and is based upon assumptions that are constructed when one thinks about a particular topic. The ideas and concepts that undergird my conceptualization of Critical Race English Education are based on the following interconnected, organized assumptions and beliefs that I possess:

- Anti-Black racism is historically and intentionally etched within social institutions (e.g., educational, healthcare, business, police system, criminal (in) justice, and political structures) and explicitly and implicitly impacts the academic and social experiences of Black children and youth.
- In order to disrupt and dismantle anti-Black racism, the structures, policies, and procedures that uphold racism, whiteness, and white supremacy must be named and unveiled.
- Educators should engage youth in humanizing racial dialogue around issues of race, anti-Blackness, white supremacy, and power. Matias (2016) states that humanizing racial dialogue "shifts the standards of humanity by providing space for the free expression of people's thoughts and emotions that are not regulated by the discourse of safety" (p. 129). On the contrary, many educators are afraid to engage youth in humanizing dialogue around race and racism because of their own lack of knowledge, fear, and discomfort.

The practices presented here grow out of Critical Race English Education, and Critical Race English Education is viewed through the Black gaze. These interconnected, organized assumptions guided my development of Critical Race English Education as a philosophical and pedagogical approach. These assumptions, as I have come to understand them, are based upon raced, classed, and gendered formations that guide my curricular and pedagogical decisions (Baszile, 2006). I recognize that these interconnected assumptions are rooted in a set of beliefs that impact how I teach ELA to secondary students and how I prepare pre-/in-service teachers to teach ELA for and with Black youth. That is, if white teachers teach ELA for and with Black youth, even in predominately white spaces, white students and communities can benefit from this knowledge. Additionally, if educators are not intentional about teaching Black texts from a critical standpoint, showcasing Blackness in a positive light, and having humanizing conversations about critical race issues and other intersections (e.g., sexuality, class, ethnicity, nationality, dis/ability, and religion), white people will not unlearn their racist ideologies or beliefs nor disrupt their own whiteness and privilege.

Let Me Be Clear

As a former secondary ELA teacher, all too often I witnessed numerous department meetings and professional development workshops where western rationality and euro-American theories and beliefs were infiltrated throughout. In turn, I also witnessed how many of the ideologies and theories that are/were present in ELA classrooms hold Black students hostage in exchange for their humanity (Haddix, 2016; Kirkland, 2013; Ladson-Billings, 2016). It is my contention that Critical Race English Education can support educators to better understand why racism and white supremacy have deep historical connections to ELA and to how we must disrupt anti-Black racism in ELA classrooms. Critical Race English Education challenges ELA teachers to positively (re)imagine ELA classrooms where Black lives, minds, and brilliance matter. Critical Race English Education helps us to center Black futures. The Black literacies tenet of Critical Race English Education is crucial because it allows us to (re)imagine how we view Black texts, culture, and knowledge. Critical Race English Education is crucial for these reasons, and these reasons should motivate us all to have an unwavering commitment to creating and maintaining classrooms as well as curricula engagements, practices, and approaches that value, love, and care for Black lives, minds, and brilliance. In these ways, we can better (re)imagine ways of teaching ELA that embrace the humanity, beauty, and strength of Blackness.

Implementing Critical Race English Education in classrooms will not work if educators and researchers are afraid to name, critique, and dismantle anti-Black racism and violence. Critical Race English Education will not work if teachers are afraid to discuss the intimate relationship among language, literacy, anti-Blackness, Blackness, and education. And, if teachers are afraid to showcase an unapologetic, unashamed, and unconditional love for Blackness and for Black people, then, Critical Race English Education will not work. Although this book speaks to ELA classroom teachers, this book is not a how-to-guide or a step-by-step model on how to be a critical race English educator. Throughout the book, I blend together theory, research, and practice to demonstrate how I have applied Critical Race English Education as a Black male educator.

But, let me be clear … you cannot teach from a Critical Race English Education perspective if you do not engage in deep soul work and explore and dismantle your own epistemological, ontological, and ideological stance before engaging in critical race practices and research. Message! This work is not for the faint at heart. We have to be willing to put our bodies and lives on the frontlines. We gotta do more than talk about it … we gotta be 'bout that life. Critical Race English Education is a "never scared" justice-oriented framework.[1] My conceptualization of Critical Race English Education is a direct link to my Black rage. When I speak of Black rage, I'm speaking of the type of rage that is a coherent and cohesive response to and/or action against anti-Black racism, violence, whiteness, patriarchy, and white supremacy. I want to be clear and note that my Black rage should not be conflated with or misconstrued for hate. I am not referring to the uncontrollable rage that leads to physical violence directed at white people by Black people (see Hooks, 1995).

This Ain't Goin' to Be Easy

Reading this book ain't goin' to be easy, and I didn't intend for it to be. If you think you're uncomfortable, imagine how Breonna Taylor's mom felt, as she witnessed the (in)justice system not charge any officers for the killing of her daughter. Imagine how Walter Wallace Jr.'s mom felt, as she watched him get shot by police officers in West Philadelphia. Nothing about Black life and Black death is easy. To love Black lives to life is not easy, especially when we are continuously met with malice and hatred. Critical Race English Education is for secondary ELA teachers, literacy educators, and English education instructors concerned with (re) imagining ELA classrooms as sites of racial justice. Because teacher preparation, pedagogies, methods, and curricula should not reflect canonical and narrow representations of language, literacy, and literature, I encourage educators to center the lived histories, language, literacies, and knowledge of Black youth to better understand their racialized and gendered experiences.

I offer classroom lessons, thematic units, sample activities, and other pedagogical and curricula practices that reconceptualize ELA pedagogies in humanizing ways that cater to the needs of students who come from racially and linguistically diverse backgrounds. While making the relationships among race, violence, racism, literacy, and equity explicit, *Critical Race English Education: New Visions, New Possibilities* also delineates the reasons why language and literacy scholars and researchers should center the language and literacy practices of racially marginalized communities in their research and scholarship. The racialized and political contexts of Black youth must be at the forefront of literacy researchers' agendas. Moreover, language and literacy researchers must take into consideration the heightened racial violence and how it impacts the literacy experiences and learning achievement of Black children (Haddix, 2016) as well as other children and youth of color (e.g., Latinx, Indigenous, and Asian).

Not only is this book for ELA teachers, language and literacy scholars, and English educators, but it is also a book for everybody. In similar and different ways, we are all impacted by anti-Black racism and violence. The societal ills that flood our nation's streets are not disconnected from the marginalization and oppression Black youth encounter in schools. In essence, this is my testimony and intellectual autobiography (Kynard, 2013). I (re)enter critical racialized moments that inform my trajectory as a Black male language and literacy scholar. Drawing from my personal experiences as a Black male navigating a racialized PreK–20 educational system, reflecting on my years teaching secondary ELA, and considering my work as a critical language and literacy scholar-activist help me to demonstrate what a Critical Race English Education workshop looks like in a secondary ELA classroom. I highlight my past educational experiences as a Black child and youth navigating the educational system. Then, I (re)enter moments from my years as an undergraduate and graduate student as well as my years as a secondary high school English language arts teacher. To better illuminate my intellectual autobiography,

I employ racial storytelling as a methodological tool that demonstrates how my past, present, and future selves are constantly in complicated dialogue with one another (Johnson, 2017).

Conjoining intellectual autobiographical writing with racial storytelling highlights how my racially related experiences from the past situate themselves in the present moment. Racial storytelling enables me to write this book in a creative way that connects to my mind, body, soul, and humanity. My goal was to write a book that goes beyond the four walls of a classroom—a book that seamlessly blends my research, theory, practice, knowledges, stories, and experiences in a non-esoteric manner. I drew upon a variety of mediums to help tell and show my stories and experiences (i.e., love letters, meditations, pictures, tables and charts, scenarios, dramatic performances, and stream of consciousness).

Love Letters, Meditations on Blackness, and a Roadmap Forward

Throughout the book, I have dispersed love letters. These love letters are my expression of love to Blackness, Black culture, and Black people. In addition, each chapter opens with a meditation on Blackness. The meditations serve as actions and practices for positive thinking and self-awareness about Blackness, given that we are living in a world where Blackness is met with malice, hatred, and hostility (Jackson, 2016). On a daily basis, Black youth enter and exit classrooms where their literacy practices and linguistic dexterity are not fully maximized.

In Chapter 1, "But It Is about Race… 'That's a Fact. Say It Louder for the People in the Back,'" I discuss how my comprehension of the prison industrial complex, school-to-prison nexus, mass incarceration, and the war on drugs derives from my personal relationship to the prison industrial complex from having a parent who was incarcerated and my schooling experiences. This chapter showcases how ELA teachers and language and literacy educators are implicated in the school-to-prison nexus. The state-sanctioned curriculum erases the experiences of Black people and renders Black lives and the Black experience as disposable.

Chapter 2, "The Other Trayvon: Anti-Black Racism and Violence against Black Lives," illustrates how the current #BlackLivesMatter Movement is intimately connected to the broader field of education and closely linked to ELA classrooms. This chapter is the impetus for the remaining chapters because I situate the ways in which Black youth encounter anti-Black violence in schools and classrooms. I place my understandings of teaching in the wake of racial violence in an anti-Black violence framework.

In Chapter 3, "Black(ness) Is, Black(ness) Ain't: Critical Race English Education," I employ Critical Race English Education as a theoretical framework to critique anti-Black racism and violence within language and literacy studies while simultaneously providing a justice-oriented framework that sheds love on the inherent beauty in Blackness. I discuss the theoretical lineage of Critical Race

English Education and the need for critical race theories and pedagogies in ELA classrooms. Oftentimes conversations pertaining to Blackness, anti-Blackness, racial violence, the school-to-prison nexus, and whiteness remain on the periphery in ELA classrooms and English education courses.

To work against the traditional and state-sanctioned curriculum, in Chapter 4, "Doin' It Wrong," I illustrate my experiences as a secondary ELA teacher, particularly how I deconstructed and (re)constructed my curriculum to center the experiences of Black youth and youth of color. This chapter builds on the previous chapter because it shows how I engage(d) in abolitionist teaching through creating a Critical Race English Education workshop model. I highlight what thematic units, lesson plans, activities, and ELA curricula look like through a Critical Race English Education workshop model. In Chapter 5, "We Have to Bring It Real Hard, Who Else Gon' Give It to 'Em?," I demonstrate how Critical Race English Education extends beyond ELA classrooms. This chapter is written as a dramatized performance. I display the family involvement and communal component of Critical Race English Education. Then, I contend that educators have to reconceptualize how we define parental involvement. I explain how ELA teachers must work to build bidirectional relationships with families and communities of color. We cannot create true and authentic justice-oriented spaces in our classrooms if we do not build with and learn from Black families and communities.

Chapter 6, "The Elephant Is ALWAYS in the Room," captures a critical family book club with family–student dyads. I analyze how the literacy uses between families and children/youth affect and respond to the intersections of identity, gender, race, language, and Blackness.

Chapter 7, "B(l)ack to the Future: Black Rage, Radical Love, and the Radical Imagination," calls for educators to imagine Black people and Black lives in the future. To create futures that center the humanity of Black people, we must operate in the radical imagination, practice radical love as an action-oriented process, and operate from the Black joy zone. Therefore, it is time for English teachers and teacher educators to bring the humanness and the humanity of Black children and youth to the forefront of their curriculum, pedagogy, methods, and research practices. It is time for us (English teachers and teacher educators) to continue to create humanizing curricula, pedagogies, methods, and research practices that subvert oppressive ELA and literacy curricula and that showcase the beauty of Blackness. It is us (literacy/English teachers and teacher educators) who should lead charge of illuminating how Black lives matter in our classrooms and in school spaces—"the tools we have at our disposal (writing, visual arts, spoken word, and other modalities more readily accepted in English and literacy classrooms) provide an outlet to discuss, critique, and dismantle this violence" (Sealey-Ruiz, 2016, p. 294). I hope the readers of this book will gain a deeper understanding of the connections between literacy, racism, and white supremacy and that they will (re) imagine the roles of English and literacy education in a time of racial turmoil and chaos for Black children and youth.

Note

1 Building upon the work of Black language scholars such as Richardson (2013) and Baker-Bell (2020), I utilized Black language to highlight my racialized and gendered experiences as well as to assist in the telling of my stories. Black language derives from the vibrant, soulful, and rich language of Black people, and it is birthed from the Black experience which is grounded in humanity, radical love, self-reliance, resistance, and freedom.

References

Anderson, J. D. (1988). *The education of Blacks in the South, 1860–1935*. Chapel Hill, NC: The University of North Carolina Press.

Baszile, D. T. (2006). Rage in the interest of Black self: Curriculum theorizing as dangerous knowledge. *Journal of Curriculum Theorizing, 22*(1), 89–98.

Bell, D. (1992). *Faces at the bottom of the well*. New York: Basic Books.

Boutte, G. S. (2015). *Educating African American students: And how are the children?* New York: Routledge.

Cridland-Hughes, S. A., & King, L. J. (2015). Killing me softly: How violence comes from the curriculum we teach. In K. Fasching-Varner & N. D. Hartlep (Eds.), *The assault on communities of Color* (pp. 67–71). Maryland: Rowman & Litttlefield.

Dumas, M. J., & Ross, K. M. (2016). "Be real Black for me": Imagining BlackCrit in education. *Urban Education, 51*, 415–442.

Foster, M. (1998). *Black teachers on teaching*. New York: The New Press.

Freire, P. (1970). *Pedagogy of the oppressed*. New York: Continuum International.

Haddix, M. (2016). *Cultivating racial and linguistic diversity in literacy teacher education: Teachers like me*. New York: Routledge.

hooks, b. (1995). *Killing rage: Ending racism*. Canada: Henry Holt and Company Inc.

Jackson, J. (2016). Meditating gunrunner speaking, part I: A Black male journey teaching in South Korea. *Educational Studies, 52*(5), 424–437.

Johnson, L. L., Jackson, J., Stovall, D., & Baszile, D. T. (2017). "Loving Blackness to Death": (Re)Imagining ELA classrooms in a time of racial chaos. *English Journal, 106*(4), 60–66.

Johnson, L. L. (2017). The racial hauntings of one Black male professor and the disturbance of the self(ves): Self-actualization and racial storytelling as pedagogical practices. *Journal of Literacy Research, 49*(4), 1–27.

Johnson, L. L. (2018). Where do we go from here?: Toward a critical race English education. *Research in the Teaching of English, 53*(2), 102–124.

Kelley, R. D. G. (2016, April). *Mike Brown's body: A meditation on war, race, & democracy* [Video file]. YouTube. Retrieved from https://www.youtube.com/watch?v=dQnw2IW9yiE&t=1042s

King, J. (2005). *Black education: A transformative research and action agenda for the new century*. New York: Routledge.

Kirkland, D. (2013). *A search past silence: Literacy, Black males, and the American dream deferred*. New York: Teachers College Press.

Knowles-Carter, B. (2019). *So much damn swag interlude. On Homecoming: The Live Album*. New York: Parkwood Entertainment.

Kynard, C. (2013). *Vernacular insurrections*. Albany, NY: State University of New York Press.

Ladson-Billings, G., & Tate, W. F. (1995). Toward a critical race theory of education. *Teachers College Record, 97*, 47–68.

Ladson-Billings, G. (2014). Culturally relevant pedagogy 2.0: a.k.a the remix. *Harvard Educational Review, 84*(1), 74–84.

Ladson-Billings, G. (2016). "#Literate lives matter": Black reading, writing, speaking, and listening in the 21st century. *Literacy Research: Theory, Method, and Practice, 65*(1), 141–151

Love, B. L. (2017). Difficult knowledge: When a Black feminist educator was too afraid to #SayHerName. *English Education, 49*(2), 192–208.

Matias, C. E. (2016). *Feeling White: Whiteness, emotionality, and education.* Boston, MA: Sense Publishers.

Maynard, R. (2017). *Policing Black lives: State violence in Canada from slavery to the present.* Canada: Fernwood Publishing.

Paris, D. (2012). Culturally sustaining pedagogy: A needed change in stance, terminology, and practice. *Educational Researcher, 41*(3), 93–97.

Richardson, E. (2013). PHD to Ph.D.: How education saved my life. Philadelphia, PA: New City Community Press.

Richardson, E., & Ragland, A. (2018). #StayWoke: The language and literacies of the #BlackLivesMatter movement. *Community Literacy Journal, 12*(2), 27–56.

Sealey-Ruiz, Y. (2016). Why Black girls' literacies matter: New literacies for a new era. *English Education, 48*(4), 290–298.

Stovall, D. O. (2015). Normalizing Black death: Michael Brown, Marissa Alexander, Dred Scott, and the apartheid state. In K. Fasching-Varner & N. D. Hartlep (Eds.), *The assault on communities of color* (pp. 67–71). Lanham, MD: Rowman & Littlefield.

Stuckey, J. E. (1990). *The violence of literacy.* Portsmouth, NH: Boynton/Cook.

Williams, P. (1987). Spirit-murdering the messenger: The discourse of fingerpointing as the law's response to racism. *University of Miami Law Review, 42*, 127–157.

Winn, M. T. (2013). Toward a restorative English education. *Research in the Teaching of English, 48*, 126–136.

Woods, J. (2019). *Baldwin. On LEGACY! LEGACY!* Chicago, IL: Jagjaguwar.

Woodson, C. G. (1933/1990). *The Mis-education of the Negro.* Trenton, NJ: Africa World Press.

LOVE LETTER I

My Dad Said I Love You … and I Said It Back

Dad,

I can recall the first time I said the words *I love you too* back to you. It was during the winter of February 2018, a few days before my 30th birthday. In that moment, I knew if I didn't say those words back to you, then I was still imprisoned by the past and my unresolved hurt. It also meant that I hadn't forgiven you for your unresolved trauma and hurt. Refusing to say the words *I love you too* would have meant that I was not fully healed from the emotional hurt from our past relationship. I understood that if I continued to carry around the emotional hurt and dislike for you, then, essentially, it meant to not like or love certain parts of myself. I didn't want to carry that baggage into my thirties, so I had to observe the situation, release it, and let it go. Prior to saying those words to you, I constantly critiqued myself for not practicing what I preached and that is showing and pouring radical love into others and loving on Blackness, even in the midst of chaos.

When I reflect on my PreK–12 schooling experiences, I think about you. When I reflect on the schooling experiences of Black youth and how many schools are designed to stifle the brilliance and beauty of Black youth, I think about you. When I reflect on the prison industrial complex and its relation to the school-to-prison nexus, I think about you. I could write about my understanding of the prison industrial complex (PIC) and its connection to the school-to-prison nexus through my experiences working with incarcerated youth, but I do not want to write a lie or a half-truth (Laymon, 2018). I have learned that writing my truths comes from the soul and requires courage.

Writing this letter has not been a painless process. I want to tell the truth—and I want that truth to be humanizing. My understanding of the PIC, mass incarceration, the war on drugs, and the school-to-prison nexus develops from my personal relationship to the PIC and mass incarceration from having a parent who was

DOI: 10.4324/9780429297052-1

incarcerated. During the early and mid-1990s and even the early 2000s, I remember you missing holidays, birthdays, church events, school-related functions, and a host of other monumental moments because of the PIC. It took me 30 years to say the words *I love you too*. I could never say those words back to you because I resented you for disengaging with me in a particular way during my childhood and youth. Even as a scholar-activist who engages in justice-oriented work, I couldn't utter the words *I love you* to my father. I never thought you didn't love me. I always knew you loved me. There were moments when you did show up. But I still held onto the anger. You called me frequently and you always ended the conversation with "I love you, son." I would reply, "peace." You never questioned me about why I never said those words back to you, and that never hindered you from reminding me how much you loved me.

I'm writing this love letter to you because I want to humanize you, dad. This is important to me; because for a good portion of my life, you and I did not have the best relationship. I do have fond memories of you. I constantly replay our last phone conversation, which took place on Wednesday, September 5, between 4:00pm and 4:30pm, a few hours before you transitioned. I know the timestamp of our conversation because the detective mentioned the calls you made on September 5 and my number was one of the last numbers on your most recent call log. Our last conversation will forever be etched in my memory because it was one of the most humanizing and organic conversations between us. I had just finished teaching. It was hotter than usual which was surprising to me because Michigan heat ain't got nothin' on South Carolina heat. Our conversation began as I walked to my car. Although the sun and the heat were on ten, you dropped a few gems that I will always carry close to me. I'm thankful you and I were able to rectify our relationship before all of this unfolded. I don't beat myself up or engage in self-flagellation because of our past issues. I understand I was in my feelings, and it was my responsibility to work through them. Our new relationship and memories outweigh the bad. You and I did not have many conversations about my years as an undergraduate or graduate student, and we did not have many conversations about my experiences teaching high school English. As I write this book, I'm writing with you in mind—I want to share my labor of love with you and provide snapshots of my journey as a scholar-activist.

I dedicate this book to you. Writing this book and love letter has been therapeutic, spiritual, and humanizing. Similarly, my book shifted when you were brutally shot and killed on September 5, 2018. Although you transitioned on September 5, the remains of your body weren't discovered until a month and a half later. My grieving process has been difficult because the person who took your life has not been found guilty. Because I'm your oldest child, I'm the one conversing with the detective about the case. However, not much conversing has been transpiring between the detectives and me. I have called and left the detective messages on his office phone and his personal device. I've even left messages with his receptionist; and I have received nothing from him. As a Critical

Race English educator and scholar, it is difficult for me to analyze this particular situation without looking at it through a racial lens. Your death has shown me how the world and others see Black lives as "another Black man gone—another tragic story that silently echoed in the background of the Black male experience" (Kirkland, 2013, p. xiii).

Witnessing firsthand how our criminal (in)justice system upholds the dehumanization of Black lives pushed me to work through my feelings toward you, which impacted my growth and understanding. As a result, my growth and understanding assisted me with being able to see that it was something bigger at play when it came to you and your relationship to the PIC. Recognizing the history of the PIC helps me to better understand the school-to-prison nexus, the criminality of Blackness, and the complexity of having a father who navigated this system. For years, I blamed and resented you for your disengagement during certain moments of my life. I remember being angry and shamed at you for being "just another statistic of Black men in prison." The media, family, and friends reminded me that only "bad" people went to prison. Buying into this pejorative narrative prompted me to overcompensate throughout my schooling experiences. I was determined to graduate high school, to attend college, and to attend graduate school. I did everything in my power not to be like you. While attending graduate school, I was introduced to brilliant Black scholars such as Dr. Carter G. Woodson. Reading Woodson's work helped me to realize how I was playing into the working of white supremacy by not fully embracing you in a loving and compassionate way.

Due to this miseducation and the absence of justice-oriented curricula and pedagogies during my schooling experiences, white supremacy and the institution of school had conditioned me to look solely at you (the individual), who was wrapped up in the machine of mass incarceration without showing how white supremacy was in collusion with your relationship to the prison industrial complex. I wonder if the nature of our relationship would have been different if I would have encountered critical race frameworks and culturally relevant, responsive, and sustaining curricula and pedagogical practices? My fourth-grade teacher, Ms. Simpkins (pseudonym), taught a lesson on slave codes and Black codes, but she talked about these violent acts as policies and laws from the past. I wonder how my understanding of (y)our relationship to the PIC might have been different if Ms. Simpkins had connected her lessons on the slave codes and Black codes to the mass incarceration and policing of Black lives during the 1990s?

Additionally, reading the work of Dr. Crystal T. Laura (2014) helped me to understand the connection and critical relationship between schools and prisons. Her compelling book, *Being Bad*, tells the story of her brother who has been impacted by the school-to-prison nexus. Reading Crystal's personal stories in relation to her brother helped me to reflect on my relationship with you.

Ultimately, I had to undergo the process of forgiveness, which aided me with releasing linked emotions that were associated with disappointment, hurt, shame, and abandonment (L. Marshall, personal communication, May 2, 2020). I had to accept you and the brokenness and trauma you carried before I even entered this world. Oprah Winfrey argues that forgiveness is about relinquishing the hope and desire that the past can be something different. Being attached to our past relationship and the negative emotions that came along with it meant that I wasn't fully human and that I wasn't fully humanizing you. A former student of mine once said, "partial liberation does not equate to full liberation" (B. Ford, personal communication, April 5, 2018). Forgiveness is about letting go, not holding onto painful memories, and ultimately, forgiveness is about being whole and free.

Oftentimes, I wonder *what would your life had been like if the school-to-prison nexus did not exist? I ask myself what did I read that you did not or what experiences did I have that you did not have?* Since you've transitioned, I have been collecting stories about you. You loved to dance and I learned that you were a member of this breakdancing group called Cosmic Dancers. I've learned that you were a talented artist, and I've witnessed some of your dope and beautiful designs and pieces. *What would your schooling experiences have been like if your teachers would have incorporated dance, art, and sports into their curriculum and pedagogical practice?* This is why Critical Race English Education is imperative because it provides future generations with a Black-centered English language arts curriculum that builds from the Black imagination and that encompasses Black humanity and demonstrates why Black lives matter inside and outside of the classroom.

Love,

Your son

In loving memory of Wade Lamar Brannon

References

Kirkland, D. (2013). *A search past silence: Literacy, Black males, and the American dream deferred.* New York: Teachers College Press.

Laura, C. T. (2014). *Being bad: My baby brother and the school-to-prison pipeline.* Teachers College Press.

Laymon, K. (2018). *Heavy.* New York: Scribner.

Marshall, L. (2020). Personal communication. May 2, 2020.

1

BUT IT IS ABOUT RACE... "THAT'S A FACT. SAY IT LOUDER FOR THE PEOPLE IN THE BACK"

Meditation #2

We have to be willing to own our feelings, particularly because we operate in a world where white rationality, patriarchy, anti-Black racism, and westernized thought illustrate emotions as a sign of weakness and portray that our emotions and feelings are detached from our truth, reasoning, body, mind, spirit, and soul.

This Is Soul Work

Real teaching comes from deep within. It transcends standards and indicators, mandated materials, lesson plans, and standardized tests. Real teaching comes from the *soul*, and teaching for liberation and human freedom is *soul* work. Since I was a child, I always possessed the urge and had the desire to become a teacher—and I knew what type of teacher I wanted to become. During my elementary school years, I was exposed to Black and white teachers. I remember sitting in classrooms where teachers basically shoved white mainstream English down our throats through teaching grammar from a skill- and drill-based practice approach. I remember being told that "avid" readers know how to pronounce words correctly and comprehend the names and sounds of letters that are affiliated with printed words. I remember my teachers' classroom libraries overflowed with white children's books and young adult literature with the exception of a few books that focused on historical Black figures such as Rosa Parks, Malcolm X, and Dr. Martin Luther King Jr., and for the most part, my secondary years mirrored my elementary years in numerous ways. Although my PreK–12 experiences were grounded in memorization, recitation, and skills-based approaches, it didn't deter me from wanting to

DOI: 10.4324/9780429297052-2

teach because I knew I would be a teacher who challenged the traditional model and ways of teaching.

Fast-forward to my undergraduate years. My passion and urge to teach grew deeper. I constantly envisioned having my own classroom and the autonomy to create and plan units, lessons, and activities that reflected the knowledge, language, literacies, histories, and culture of youth who were like me. At my undergraduate institution, secondary education majors had to major in a particular subject area (i.e., science, math, social studies, or English) and minor in education. We had to apply for a 5th year master's program. As an English major with a concentration in secondary education, there were required courses I had to complete in order to be admitted to the master's program. One course in particular, "Teaching Middle and High School English," was a foundational course that introduced me to the reading and writing workshop model, thematic unit planning, the teaching of young adult literature, and how to put it into conversation with canonical texts. It redefined my conceptualization of what could be considered a text.

This course was taught by Dr. Hendrickson, a monolingual, middle-aged white woman. She taught and demonstrated to me the art and structure of teaching. She pushed back against traditional paradigms and taught from a social constructivist approach. Dr. Hendrickson believed that young people construct their own understandings and knowledge of the world through deep reflection, connection, questioning, and real-world problem solving. Although this was a few steps above the traditional paradigms I learned about in my previous educational courses, there was something still lacking from her teaching practices and methods.

My relationship with Dr. Hendrickson was a real struggle. On the one hand, her emphasis on the importance of student choice and valuing student knowledge helped me to understand the art of teaching and learning. On the other hand, the absence of race talk and the partiality of sociocultural and feminist theories created an ongoing dilemma. Dr. Hendrickson's social constructivist approaches to the classroom were taught through the white gaze—it was culturally irrelevant. My soul still longed for the experiences, voices, language, literacies, histories, and knowledges of Black people, but they were nowhere to be found.

Something Inside So Strong

For one of our major assignments, Dr. Hendrickson had us create a thematic unit plan on a canonical text of our choice. I was disinterested in creating a thematic unit on *The Great Gatsby*, *The Odyssey*, *Huckleberry Finn*, *Julius Caesar*, or any of the other texts that are a part of the typical high school canon, written from the white gaze. Instead, I selected Lorraine Hansberry's play, *A Raisin in the Sun*. I wanted to select an author who resembled me. An author who reflected my experiences. An author who wrote from the soul. I understood all too well how Black authors and texts are marginalized in many academic spaces from PreK–12 education to higher educational spaces. In these spaces, Black people are constantly forced to read white authors. Black authors are an afterthought or secondary texts.

As stated above, my education courses did not draw upon critical paradigms such as culturally relevant pedagogy, culturally relevant teaching, critical race theory, or critical race pedagogy. However, I understood that if I wanted to be an educator who centered the Black experience, I had to fight against anti-Black racism through resistance, self-determination, being justice-minded, and taking action by being, in the eyes of some, radical in my choices. To illustrate, for one of my lessons, I explored how the utilization of African American Language (AAL), or what I now refer to as Black Language, in *A Raisin in the Sun* impacts the meaning of the text.

Dr. Hendrickson did not introduce my class to Black Language. I did not know this term even existed, but I knew as Black people we had our own distinct language. Therefore, I wanted to create a unit that would introduce my future students to the legitimacy and richness of Black Language through *A Raisin in the Sun*. I stumbled across the term AAL while researching *A Raisin in the Sun*, specifically exploring the language of the characters in the play. I created a lesson through which the youth would analyze AAL as it is used in both *A Raisin in the Sun* and *Good Times*, an American sitcom that aired in the 1970s and was based on an impoverished Black family living in Chicago. As a speaker of Black Language, it was important for me to shed a positive light on Black Language because so often in classrooms and society at large, Black youth and adults are forced to black out our language and erase our linguistic identity through privileging white mainstream English (Baker-Bell, 2018; Boutte, 2015).

At the time, I didn't possess the critical language or applications to name the type of educator I envisioned becoming; however, there was an energetic force that came from deep within and it pushed me toward more critical work. I have engaged in deep soul work and I now know that it was something spiritual moving me. The Universe and my ancestors were preparing me as my past self was in critical conversation with my present self, and both were in conversation with my future self, which primed me for where I am now. I was on a different wavelength and frequency than Dr. Hendrickson and my other white peers. Not only were my ancestors living and resting within me, but also I was drawing upon my own set of language and literacies that lived within me.

The Block Is Hot: The Policing of Black Lives in and out of Classrooms

I met Donovan a week after finishing my undergraduate program. I had just begun my master's program in secondary English education. I walked across the stage on Saturday, May 8, 2010, and I started my graduate program two days later. My first graduate course, which focused on the foundations of reading instruction, required that I work one-on-one with a "struggling" reader. The instructor whom I mentioned above, Dr. Hendrickson, was also the instructor for this course. She created a partnership with the Detention of Juvenile Justice (DJJ). Twice a week, roughly 17–18 white pre-service teachers as well as me and a Black female pre-service teacher were sent there to "help" and "save" *struggling* Black male youth. Before I had any contact with my literacy partner, Donovan, Dr. Hendrickson had already labeled him and the other Black males as *struggling* readers. To name Donovan and the other incarcerated youth there as *struggling* readers connoted that all Black males who are incarcerated "struggle" with reading and do not already have textual and literacy proficiencies. To use the word *struggling* underscores deficit thinking and showcases incarcerated Black youth as deficient and anti-intellectual.

I quickly discovered, as I had anticipated, that these Black males were highly literate and did not need nobody to save them. Donovan explained how much he loved to read and write poetry. He delineated his reading process—for example, he explained how his mom taught him active reading strategies such as context clues, visualization, inference, and prediction. He talked about how much he enjoyed reading young adult novels written by Sharon Draper and Walter Dean Myers. I can recall Donovan explaining his disdain for *The Scarlet Letter* which was a mandated reading in his ELA course. He specifically stated, "I couldn't relate to the main character in *The Scarlet Letter*. Hester, the main character, walked down the stairs and shot somebody … and, I will never murder anybody." Donovan's powerful words, *I will never murder anybody*, touched my core. As a Black male, I understood Donovan's sentiments—Black males get erroneously accused of being criminals, violent, and murderers. Donovan activated his voice to let the world know that he would never physically take another human being's life. During our three weeks together, Donovan reminded me that he is a reader and that "reading was a good feeling." He reminded me that he is somebody's child, a father, a writer, a poet, and human.

Connecting and learning from Donovan strengthened my realization that we, the pre-service teachers, were the ones who were struggling. We were taught westernized and eurocentric reading strategies and assessments to "teach" reading to Black males. For example, we had to conduct reading interviews based on narrow and eurocentric models of what counts as text, perform a Miscue Analysis, and create and administer a strategic reading intervention. These positivistic paradigms lacked the social, cultural, racial, and linguistic intersections that influence and inform Black youth's language and literacy practices. I didn't have the critical language to name it in that moment; however, because of the Black experiences, I knew applying these white theories and practices to Black youth was problematic. Also, I knew most of my white peers would take these learned understandings about "struggle" and "intervention" and enact them in the form of pedagogical violence on the Black youth they would encounter inside and outside of classrooms. I couldn't help but to question *what ways their (the pre-service teachers) assumed knowledge would engineer the physical and spiritual-murder of Black youth.* It is no secret that white and westernized knowledge, language, notions of literacy, and ways of being permeate ELA classrooms and the educational arena at large. This should not come as a surprise, seeing that the teaching force is largely comprised of white, monolingual, middle-class, able-bodied, Protestant, and cisgender females.

The profuse number of white teachers in classrooms creates a cultural, racial, ethnic, and linguistic mismatch and disconnect between white teachers and Black youth. In fact, the racial and linguistic disharmony between white teachers and Black youth perpetuates the surveillance and policing of Black lives (Samudzi & Anderson, 2018). The policing and surveillance of Black lives that happen in the streets are wedded to the policing and hyper-surveillance of Blackness that unfold in classrooms and within school buildings. Maynard (2017) explains,

> Policing, indeed, describes not only cops on their beat, but also the past and present surveillance of Black women by social assistance agents, the over-disciplining and racially targeted expulsion of Black children and youth in schools, and the acute surveillance and detention of Black migrants by border control agencies.
>
> *(p. 7)*

Within the institution of schools, teachers often surveil, police, discipline, and control Black youth because of the heavy presence of white supremacy.

The over-surveillance of Black lives shows us that not only is the block hot within Black communities, but also the block is hot within PreK–12 classrooms. The phrase *the block is hot* is Black Language that communicates that the police are on the block and they are up to no good. The block is also hot inside of many undergraduate and graduate-level teacher education courses. For instance, with my graduate experiences working with incarcerated youth, I am now aware that the paradigms, frameworks, and pedagogies we encountered did not critique whiteness, name white supremacy, evaluate the school-to-prison nexus, or shed light on the beauty of Blackness (Doyle, 2018). It was evident that my white peers were learning how to teach through observing our instructor of the course, Dr. Hendrickson. Many of the white pre-service teachers from my program learned how to teach through what Lortie (1975/2002) calls the apprenticeship of observation, which has a tremendous impact on pre-service teachers. Pre-service teachers enter their teacher education programs, practicums, and internships with narrow constructions of teaching based on their former experiences as PreK–20 students who have watched predominately white female teachers. Many pre-service teachers enter their teacher education programs with false ideologies and perceptions about education that are deeply rooted in whiteness.

Take, for instance, one of my colleagues/friend, Dr. Jennifer Doyle, who was in the same secondary English education graduate cohort that I was in. In her dissertation, Doyle (2018) critiques her past, present, and future selves, institutionalized racism, and whiteness in relation to being a white and former pre-service candidate, in-service teacher, and graduate student who attended a predominately white institution. In this autoethnographic account, she reflects on her experiences with Dr. Hendrickson as an undergraduate and graduate student. She states:

> I learned how to be a teacher from watching Dr. Hendrickson (she taught us methods and strategies as a teacher, by having us, as future teachers, act as the students engaging in methods). Moreover, both of my coaching teachers were white women, as was Pat, the other professor in the MT program. But I most wanted to be like Dr. Hendrickson. Just like I most wanted to be like my mother as a child, my first teacher. I emulated both of them. I learned how to play the game of whiteness from both of them. Both of them were feminists, so they knew how to "play the game"—which I now take as playing the game of patriarchy—but they were also playing the game of whiteness. And maybe they didn't know it. What a dangerous game—white patriarchy! A game in which I was learning just by observing them.

Jen's analysis of being implicated in the apprenticeship of observation demonstrates the centrality of whiteness. It sheds light on how the educational arena continues to sew the seed of whiteness through planting pathologizing and criminalizing depictions about what Black is and what Black ain't (Riggs & Atkinson, 1995). Bryan (2017), who extrapolates the apprenticeship of observation to the school-to-prison pipeline, argues that teachers erroneously discipline Black males which contributes to Black males' connection to the school-to-prison pipeline (what I refer to as the school-to-prison nexus). Rather than looking at schools as places that can lead to prison, Stovall (2018) surmises that schools function as prisons that reflect the carceral state. He asserts:

> If you think about a place where students are punished if they do not walk on demarcated lines in the floor, are required to remain silent during lunch, required to wear uniforms (including clear backpacks), subject to random searches, and are fined for being out of uniform, this place is not "leading" you to prison. Instead, we should understand that space as an operative prison, with the main difference being that you are allowed to go home every afternoon.
>
> *(p. 56)*

Prison is a dehumanizing, dilapidating place that was built to uphold white supremacy and capitalism. It was created to enslave Black people, erase our historical and contemporary knowledge about who we are, and to put a cap on our freedom. In a like manner, the traditional and narrow conception of "school" should be viewed in the same light. Before I fully unpack how the conception of school connects to the prison industrial complex, I want to first work through understanding the complexities of the PIC system.

The Prison Industrial Complex

The PIC is a capitalistic beast that is comprised of racialized and oppressive structures, policies, and systems (Peterson, 2016) that incarcerate millions of Black, Brown, Indigenous, and queer people and immigrant communities. To sustain the disposability and incarceration of people and communities of color, in this particular case Black people, the PIC has an intimate relationship with private corporations, lobbyists, politicians, the government, and the educational arena. These big corporations share a set of ideologies that intersect and sustain the mass incarceration of Black lives through surveillance, policing, and imprisonment. To illustrate, corporations such as Allstate Insurance Company, Blue Cross and Blue Shield Corporation, Liberty Mutual Insurance, GEICO, State Farm Insurance, Aramark Food Service, Nationwide Insurance, Procter & Gamble, Fruit of the Loom, AT&T, BellSouth Telecommunications, Sprint, Verizon Communications, The Boeing Company, United Airlines, AutoZone, Mary Kay Cosmetics, Microsoft Corporation, Wal-Mart, and countless more (Peterson, 2016) feed the PIC for economic profitability and social gain. It is important to note that many educational institutions have partnerships with these private companies such as Aramark, a food service provider.

Aramark has partnerships with over 380 US PreK–12 school districts, and it has connections to numerous colleges and universities (Kelkar, 2019). Although Aramark is a billion-dollar corporation, it does not make its money only from its educational business partnership with schools but also from its connection with private prisons. According to Oceguera and Sager (2019), Aramark functions in over 600 correctional facilities within the US and Canada. Inmates have complained and filed suit about food safety and severe health issues that have transpired from eating non-nutritious meals. Further, inmates have activated their voices and have taken action through participating in national hunger strikes and protesting against correctional facilities' partnerships with Aramark. Kelkar (2019) states that Aramark has a longstanding history of oppressing prisoners and serving them unpleasant meals. Aramark also benefits from the labor and enslavement of Black lives through employing inmates to handle food services, laundry, and janitorial services (Kelkar, 2019). Corporations like Aramark feed the PIC by paying prisons for the labor of inmates which speaks to what Alexander (2010) refers to as modern-day slavery. A major business such as Aramark makes millions to handle government operations.

To illustrate, at one point, food was prepared by government employees and often, inmates would assist the government employees. However, many of these government jobs have been cut because of the billions of dollars that private businesses accumulate from cheap labor which utilizes inmate labor. Because

Aramark serves as a leading food provider for many correctional institutions and builds its company off the enslavement of predominantly Black and Brown people, institutions such as New York University, Arizona State University, University of California, and University of Central Florida have pushed back against and broken ties with Aramark. Students have protested against Aramark's relationship to the PIC and argued for institutions to end their partnerships with the food service provider because of Aramark's upliftment of mass incarceration. I am in agreement with student activist, justice-oriented scholars, and prison abolitionists that the educational system needs to cut ties with private businesses such as Aramark and say no more. By the same token, educational systems and national education organizations have to be more critical about the vendors we are funding. Oftentimes, these big businesses have their hands in the PIC and school systems are supporting them by utilizing these corporations for food services, janitorial services, and health insurance. Educational systems should not be funding anything or anyone who funds the PIC. Period. And while many universities are breaking ties with Aramark, we need to be side-eyeing insurance companies who also have their hands in the PIC because many school districts and universities have business partnerships with them as well.

By any means necessary, white supremacy works to continue the policing of Black lives. Through the historical assault against Black lives and the state of colonization, the enslavement of Black folks has served as economic, physical, spiritual, psychological, and humanistic exploitation (Johnson et al., 2017; Matias, 2016). The past and present enslavement and policing of Black people are clothed in the prison industrial complex. It should not come as a surprise that corporations are making billions of dollars from federal and state prison facilities through the criminality of Blackness. The PIC and the criminality of Blackness have a longstanding history with Black folks. These are not new concepts or new realities—they have existed since the enslavement and colonization of Black people across the African Diaspora, the earliest form of the prison industrial complex traced back to Africa to what are known as "slave castles" and dungeons. The confinement, surveillance, and dehumanization of Black people originated prior to Africans being forced to come to America (Peterson, 2016). In Ghana, West Africa, as one of many examples, Africans were brutalized, branded, and oppressed before being shackled and physically and mentally abused on the horrid Middle Passage. Peterson (2016) contends that "the slave castles of West Africa, like the penitentiaries of 19th-century America, had an imposing architecture: towers for surveillance; dungeons of various shapes, sizes, and purposes, some for the sole intent of confining and starving 'unruly' Africans to death" (p. 38). As for corporations today, the policing and bondage of Black people provided economic gain for the colonizers and enslavers who had business partnerships with manufacturing and agriculture companies that benefited from the forced labor, institutional racism, and confinement of Black lives (Maynard, 2017; Peterson, 2016).

"Just Say No" and the War on Drugs

Reflecting on the past and current realities pertaining to the criminality of Blackness and my relationships to the PIC has prompted me to (re)enter my schooling experiences. I now know and understand how schools all too often can serve as institutions that miseducate (Woodson, 1933) Black children and youth about the PIC, the disproportionate arrest rates of Black children, youth, and adults, and the over-policing of Black lives through the routine of pathologization and criminalization of Black people (Maynard, 2017).

During my fifth-grade year and through all of middle school, I remember the school district mandating teachers to dedicate 40–50 minutes a week for students to engage in Drug Abuse Resistance Education (D.A.R.E.) curriculum. D.A.R.E. is a police-led program that teaches youth how to resist peer pressure and live drug- and violence-free lives (https://dare.org/about/). For months, local police officers, the teachers of the D.A.R.E. curriculum, visited our classrooms to discuss how drugs were ruining communities, schools, and the nation. The local police officers preached and promoted Nancy Reagan's slogan of "Just Say No." In addition to focusing on drugs, the police officers would share stories with us about Black-on-Black crime in Black communities and gang violence. Through deficit drug prevention and blame-the-victim rhetoric, the police officers preached that we should be kind, be obedient, be respectful, be smart, and be a winner. In other words, if we performed these characteristics and just said no to drugs, then, we could have a taste of the "American Dream." We were mandated to take quizzes and tests; after a few months, we received a certificate upon completion of the program. What I find interesting yet unsurprising is how Nixon, Reagan, and Clinton were exalted and sanctified as heroes and angels when discussing drug prevention and violence. In actuality, these political figures were being praised for their instrumental roles in permeating anti-Blackness through the policing of Black lives, surveilling Black lives by drug law enforcement, and through the unjust laws and policies that detained and confined Black communities. At the same time, white youth were selling and using drugs with little, if any, punishment in affluent suburbs across the country (Alexander, 2010). The untold stories, truths, and secrets about Nixon, Reagan, and Clinton's relationship to the mass incarceration of Black folks were nicely tucked away behind the majoritarian narrative of associating Blackness with criminality.

According to Peterson (2016), the Nixon presidential campaign encouraged and embodied the rhetoric of "law and order." Nixon believed the social and political uprisings and resistance from the Civil Rights Movement were causing *terror* and *chaos* across the nation. President Richard Nixon also believed that the sit-ins, protests, freedom rides, and the shouting of "I'm Black and I'm proud!" were the roots and causes of this nation's social unrest and absence of law and order. Love (2019) writes, "Nixon's racist, combative, state-sanctioned, violent tactics killed and criminalized dark folx in order to appeal to White voters" (p. 46).

Nixon laid the foundation for the war on drugs. During his presidency, he announced that drug abuse was "public enemy number one." However, it was the presidency of Ronald Reagan that moved the war on drugs from a slogan to action through incarcerating a large mass of Black folks for nonviolent drug offenses. The Reagan administration employed a strategic media campaign around the crack epidemic that surfaced in the 1980s. Alexander (2010) declared that,

> Almost overnight, the media was saturated with images of black "crack whores," crack dealers," and "crack babies"—images that seemed to confirm the worst negative racial stereotypes about impoverished inner-city residents. The media bonanza surrounding the "new demon drug" helped to catapult the War on Drugs from an ambitious federal policy to an actual war.
>
> *(p. 5)*

It is no secret that the war on drugs was and still remains a genocidal charge against Black lives. Since the beginning of the war on drugs slogan and actual war, Black people got wind that the CIA was smuggling and bringing crack and other drugs into Black neighborhoods and communities (see Alexander, 2010; Peterson, 2016; Maynard, 2017). In fact, the genocidal charge stemmed from the stark racial disparities and the disproportionate rates of drug crime between people of color and white folks which placed a massive number of Black people in prison.

The genocidal charge stemmed from the dehumanizing and uncivil encounters between military-style raids conducted by SWAT teams and police officers which resulted in police bustin' into Black people's places of residence, usually in the middle of the night, "throwing grenades, shouting, and pointing guns and rifles at anyone inside, often including young children" (Alexander, 2010, p. 75). These drug raids have taken the lives of many innocent Black children, youth, and adults while white affluent drug users and dealers were typically either ignored or let off with light, not life-ending sentences. In 1980, there were 50,000 people incarcerated for nonviolent drug law offenses and by 1997 that number rose to 400,000 (Peterson, 2016). Neither the Republicans nor the Democrats made any attempts to eradicate the PIC, mass incarceration, or the war on drugs; if anything, they moved expeditiously to further the incarceration, confinement, and policing of Black lives.

In like manner, President Clinton continued to carry the agenda of mass incarceration and the war on drugs through his "get tough" movement on the Black community (Alexander, 2010). The Clinton administration invested $16 billion dollars to expand the prison system through increasing state and local police forces and expanding the development of prisons. Furthermore, "The Clinton administration intensified the 'War on Dark People' with the 1994 crime bill, which required federal prisoners to serve 85 percent of their sentence before they could be eligible for parole" (Love, 2019, p. 60). In the same light, Hilary Clinton perpetuated the "War on Dark People" when she dehumanized young Black males by labeling them as "superpredators." In 1996, at Keene State College in Keene, New Hampshire, Hilary Clinton declared:

> We need to take these people on, they are often connected to big drug cartels, they are not just gangs of kids anymore. They are often the kinds of kids that are called superpredators. No conscience. No empathy. We can talk about why they ended up that way but first we have to bring them to heel.
>
> *(C-SPAN, 1996, Superpredators)*

Hilary's depiction of Black youth paints Black children as inhuman and soul-less people. The pathologizing rhetoric and (mis)reading of Black youth are ingrained in the hearts and minds of government officials, politicians, police officers, lawyers, and judges. Take, for example, in 2009, in Wilkes-Barre, PA, two judges were found guilty in accepting over $2 million for erroneously convicting Black youth regardless of whether they were guilty, innocent, or how serious their assumed offense was (Peterson, 2016). The depiction of Black children and youth as "superpredator" had seeped into courtrooms just as it seeped into classrooms, schools reflecting the carceral state wedding both institutions together.

Surveillance of Black Youth in Schools

Black youth are surveilled and criminalized within educational spaces. The spirit of the carceral state travels throughout the halls of many schools across the US. In 2015, I visited an urban high school in Cincinnati, OH. Before crossing the threshold to enter the school, I was greeted with metal detectors and a police officer. To the right of me, I was met with bright red, white, and blue colors of the American flag and to the left of me, there was a cardboard silhouette of a Black male youth with his hands raised in the "hands up don't shoot" position. As I continued to walk down the hall, I discovered an elevator with the following warning: "Staff use only, unauthorized use by student/s will result in five days of suspension." On a daily basis, in many schools across the nation, youth are greeted with metal detectors, unfair suspensions, law enforcement officers, school lockdowns, and arrests for miniscule infractions. Time after time, Black youth are depicted as uneducable, animalistic, hypersexual, and criminals.

On February 4, 2019, at Lawton Chiles Middle Academy in Lakeland, FL, an 11-year-old Black male student was arrested for allegedly becoming disruptive while refusing to stand for the Pledge of Allegiance. According to Simon (2019), the substitute teacher asked the student to stand for the pledge, but the student refused to stand for the pledge because he believed that the United States is a discriminatory place that has an ongoing history with the mistreatment of Black lives. Following the Black male youth's statement, the substitute called for an administrator and school police officer. In the school resource officer's report, he stated the school district allows for the freedom of expression; however, they do not condone the disturbance of a "peaceful classroom where *all* students can learn" (https://www.cnn.com/2019/02/18/us/florida-pledge-of-allegiance-al tercation-arrest/index.html). Even though the school district has a written state-ment about students not being required to stand for the pledge, the young Black child was arrested because he did not comply with the school administrator and officer's request to leave the classroom. He was arrested for causing a "disturbance" in the classroom and resisting an officer without violence and was transported to a juvenile detention center (Simon, 2019).

Black Youth and the School-to-Prison Nexus

I am in alignment with Bryan (2017) that Black children and youth are ear-marked for unfair, disproportionate school disciplining through the policy of zero tolerance. Zero-tolerance policies are unharmonious and intolerant. Indeed, the unfair discipline of Black lives upholds the school-to-prison nexus. As a result of this, schools create policies that push Black youth out of schools and into juvenile detention centers, immigration detention centers, and prisons. Zero-tolerance policies were originally created in response to mass shootings in schools and to deter students from bringing weapons to schools; however, Black youth have been heavily impacted by zero-tolerance policies and are rep-rimanded without second thought ("Shared Justice," 2019). Black youth are sus-pended and expelled for minor infractions at higher rates than their white peers which underpins and perpetuates the pathological fear of Blackness and Black lives. According to the United Negro College Funds (2019), Black youth are 3.8 times as likely to undergo out-of-school suspensions as opposed to white students. In a like manner, Black youth are 2.3 times as likely to experience a referral to school law enforcement or undergo school-related arrest as opposed to white students.

To illuminate, Sealey-Ruiz (2016) and Love (2019) assert that Black girls are entering schools during a time of mass incarceration, punitive zero policies, and dehumanizing treatment from school resource officers, teachers, and staff. Black girls are often stereotyped and (mis)read as loud, angry, rude, and hypersexual which makes it difficult for Black girls to maneuver school spaces because they are frequently suspended and expelled because of such deficit, subjective labels (Crenshaw et al., 2015). Black girls are rarely provided the spaces and opportuni-ties just to be Black girls. Love (2019) contends that Black girls often encounter "age compression" which is an occurrence in Black girlhood because Black girls' childhood and youth are taken from them because society sees them as Black women. This notion of "age compression" can be extrapolated and applied to the lives of Black boys. Bryan (2017) and Ladson-Billings (2011) explicate that at an early age Black boys are often labeled as "men," and their childhood and inno-cence are ripped from them.

In addition, Black youth who are members of the LGBTQIA+ community encounter violence, bullying, sexual assault, sexual harassment, and discriminatory treatment and are pushed out of schools at an alarming rate (Maynard, 2017). Equally, Black youth with disabilities face numerous challenges in schools and are pushed out of schools and encounter multiple forms of systemic discrimination and oppression. Maynard (2017) writes that "The Ontario *Safe Schools Act* (2001-2008), which created harsher and more punitive suspension and expulsion policies until it was repealed, resulted in a massive spike of expulsions that impacted Black students and students with disabilities most severely" (p. 225).

In addition to the intersection of race, gender, and (dis)ability, Black migrant students who are undocumented continue to be erased and denied in schools. There have been incidents in schools where undocumented Black migrant youth have received punitive treatment and are punished for not having documented papers which have led to the detainment and deportation of them and their families (Maynard, 2017). Immigrant children as young as three years old are being mandated to court for their own deportation hearings without having a parent or guardian present (Jewett & Luthra, 2018). In short, the creation of these harsh and dehumanizing policies and conditions directly impact Black youths' opportunities for academic, emotional, and social success in schools.

In light of our most recent racial and political climate, I believe it is crucial for teachers, particularly in this case, ELA teachers, language and literacy scholars, and English educators, to stand against issues of PIC, mass incarceration, and the school-to-prison nexus. We have to continually ask ourselves: *What is our role in this ongoing struggle for justice?* It is necessary to understand that literacy is not detached from issues of racism, anti-Blackness, or xenophobia—literacy mirrors our racial, cultural, and geographical contexts. If the fields of language and literacy studies and English education remain silent on the mass incarceration of Black lives, the killing of unarmed Black people, and the detainment of children and youth from their families, it renders us complicit in the sustainment of racial injustice. The teaching of English language arts is linked to the PIC and the school-to-prison nexus when we (as educators) do not critically build on the language and literacy practices that Black youth bring to classrooms. Indeed, the *block remains hot* when we provide Black youth with texts where their ways of existing and being in the world are (mis)read, negated, and erased. This constitutes elements of mediocre language and literacy instruction, critical components of the school-to-prison nexus (Winn & Behizadeh, 2011).

Engaging Black youth in culturally unresponsive curricula and pedagogical practices can potentially push out Black youth by leading them to disengage with reading, writing, and speaking and the schooling process in general. Historically, literacy has been frequently defined as the, "ability to read and write. The content, context, and purpose of reading were unimportant; literacy was conceptualized as a neutral, decontextualized skill" (Winn & Behizadeh, 2011, p. 150) when in fact a view of white supremacy was and is taught in those such instructional practices. Thus, it is important to understand that language and literacy education is a political act and that equitable teaching means educating youth about the working of anti-Blackness while shedding light on what Blackness is, its heritage, language, beauty as critical components in disrupting the school-to-prison nexus. I believe this type of anti-racist education can increase youth abilities to critically read and question the world, understand the complexity of Blackness, and utilize their language and literacy practices to create and humanize.

School Abolition and Abolitionist Teaching

I bring this chapter to a close knowing that, as shown in the earlier part of this chapter, I have always possessed this fire and riot in my soul (Baszile, 2006). Before I knew the term the radical imagination, the spirit of the radical imagination lived within me. Stovall (2018) argues the radical imagination "seeks to understand the world in its current state while vehemently working with others to change the current condition" (p. 51). Embodying the radical imagination compels me to engage in praxis that takes action to eradicate a dehumanizing system that impedes the chances of creating a more just and equitable world (Johnson, 2017). As a scholar-activist, embracing the radical imagination has pushed me to envision a world free of anti-Blackness, police violence, the prison industrial complex, and economic deprivation (Johnson et al., 2017). This notion of the radical imagination stems from prison abolitionism—the abolitionist believes and argues that the prison system needs to be abolished as the main system of tackling social ills (Davis, 2015). Abolition isn't just about eradicating the buildings of prisons, but it also pertains to critiquing and overturning the world we currently live in because the PIC and schools sustain and maintain violence, confinement, and the disposability of Black lives.

I am in agreement with Davis (2015) that embracing an abolitionist vision means that we must construct models that depict how we want to live in the future. According to a national organization, Critical Resistance, being an abolitionist, "means developing practical strategies for taking small steps that move us toward making our dreams real and that lead us all to believe that things really could be different. It means living this vision in our daily lives." In a similar vein, scholars such as Stovall (2018) and Wun (2015) call for educators to embrace the spirit of school abolition which is similar to prison abolition. School abolition aims to eradicate an educational system that is deeply rooted in white supremacy, capitalism, and dehumanization. In order to do this, school abolition does not necessarily mean the destruction of school buildings—in this instance, school abolition calls for educators to (re)imagine schools because the traditional model of "school" centers on order, compliance, violence, and dehumanization which continuously unfold in school buildings. School abolition focuses on disrupting the pathologizing narrative and belief that Black lives are disposable and that Blackness connotes criminality.

Stovall (2018) writes,

> In the same vein, "school" abolition should also be a long-term goal, centered in the activity of students, parents, teachers, and activists to revisit and build an abolitionist future in education. School abolition is connected to abolitionist teaching, which is grounded in joy, radical love, tenacity, humanization, and creativity (Love, 2019). Abolition, in this sense is "not a utopian dream, but a necessity"
>
> *(Meiners, 2011, p. 5, as cited in Stovall, 2018, p. 55)*

In like manner, I am reminded of the spirit of Love (2019) who calls for "Abolitionist teaching" which is imbued with radical love, Black joy, hope, resistance, tenacity, freedom, imagination, creativity, and humanization. Before I entered a classroom, I channeled the spirit of abolitionist teaching, as a result of my lived and racialized experiences. I understood that the past and modern-day ELA classrooms and the conditions of ELA classrooms (i.e., decentering Black literary voices and writers, privileging white mainstream English, inexperienced teachers, and overcrowded classrooms) had everything to do with the anatomy of schools and not an oversight from the students or families (Stovall, 2020). Before I entered a classroom, I was constantly freedom dreaming (Kelley, 2002) and carrying the radical imagination of Black thinkers, revolutionaries, and community members as fearless acts of love to attain a better world.

References

Alexander, M. (2010). *The new jim crow: Mass incarceration in the age of colorblindness*. New York: The New Press.

Baker-Bell, A. (2018). I can switch my language, but I can't switch my skin: What teachers must understand about linguistic racism. In E. Moore, A. Michael, & M. Penick-Parks (Eds.), *The guide for White women who teach Black boys*. (pp. 97–107). Thousand, Oaks: CA: Corwin Press.

Baszile, D. T. (2006). Rage in the interest of Black self: Curriculum theorizing as dangerous knowledge. *Journal of Curriculum Theorizing, 22*(1), 89–98.

Boutte, G. S. (2015). *Educating African American students: And how are the children?* New York, NY: Routledge.

Bryan, N. (2017). White teachers' role in sustaining the school-to-prison pipeline: Recommendations for Teacher Education. *Urban Review, 49*(2), 326–345.

Crenshaw, K., Ocen, P., & Nanda, J. (2015). *Black Girls Matter: Pushed out, overpoliced, and underprotected*. New York: African American Policy Forum & Center for Intersectionality and Social Policy Studies.

C-Span. (2016, February 25). 1996: Hillary Clinton on "superpredators". Retrieved from https://www.youtube.com/watch?v=j0uCrA7ePno

Davis, A. (2015). *Freedom is a constant struggle: Ferguson, Palestine, and the foundations of a Movement*. Chicago, IL: Haymarket Books.

D.A.R.E. (2021, February 1). D.A.R.E. https://dare.org/

Doyle, J. L. (2018). Becoming a sailor: A (critical) analytic autoethnographic account of navigating tensions as a 'woke' white woman working for racial justice. (Doctoral dissertation). Retrieved from https://scholarcommons.sc.edu/etd/4740

Jewett, C., & Luthra, S. (2019, June 7). From crib to court: Trump administration summons immigrant infants. Retrieved from https://khn.org/news/from-crib-to-court-trump-administration-summons-immigrant-infants/

Johnson, L. L., Jackson, J., Stovall, D., & Baszile, D. T. (2017). "Loving Blackness to Death": (Re)Imagining ELA classrooms in a time of racial chaos. *English Journal, 106*(4), 60–66.

Johnson, L. L. (2017). The racial hauntings of one Black male professor and the disturbance of the self(ves): Self-actualization and racial storytelling as pedagogical practices. *Journal of Literacy Research, 49*(4), 1–27.

Kelkar, K. (2019, December 13). Prison strike organizers to protest food giant Aramark. *PBS News Hour Weekend.* Retrieved from https://www.pbs.org/newshour/nation/prison-strike-protest-Aramark.

Kelley, R. D. G. (2002). *Freedom dreams: The Black radical imagination.* Boston, MA: Beacon Press.

Ladson-Billings, G. (2011). Boyz to men? Teaching to restore Black boys' childhood. *Race, Ethnicity, and Education, 14*(1) 7–15.

Lortie, D. (1975/2002). *Schoolteacher: A sociological study.* Chicago, IL: University of Chicago Press.

Maynard, R. (2017). *Policing Black lives: State violence in Canada from slavery to the present.* Nova Scotia: Fernwood Publishing.

Love, B. L. (2019). *We want to do more than survive: Abolitionist teaching and the pursuit of educational freedom.* Boston, MA: Beacon Press.

Matias, C. E. (2016). *Feeling white: whiteness, emotionality, and education.* Boston, MA: Sense Publishers.

Meiners, E. (2011). Ending the school-to-prison pipeline/building abolition futures. *The Urban Review, 43*(1), 547–567.

Oceguera, E., & Sager, M. (2019, December 13). The prison Industry on your campus. Retrieved from https://medium.com/@Investigate/the-prison-industry-on-your-campus-616a856e8ff0

Peterson, J. B. (2016). *Prison industrial complex: For beginners.* A For Beginners Documentary Comic Book.

Riggs, M., & Atkinson, N. (1995). *Black is..Black ain't* [DVD, Video file].

Samudzi, Z., & Anderson, W. C. (2018). *As Black as resistance: Finding the conditions for liberation.* Chico, CA: AK Press.

Sealey-Ruiz, Y. (2016). Why Black girls' literacies matter: New literacies for a new era. *English Education, 48*(4), 290–298.

Simon, D. (2019, December 17). Florida student arrested for disturbance after he refused to participate in the pledge of allegiance. 17 December 2019. Retrieved from https://www.cnn.com/2019/02/18/us/florida-pledge-of-allegiance-altercation-arrest/index.html

Shared Justice. (2019, June 7). Retrieved from http://www.sharedjustice.org/domesticjustice/2017/12/21/zero-tolerance-policies-and-the-school-to-prison-pipeline

Stovall, D. (2017). Freedom as aspirational and fugitive: A humble response. *Equity & Excellence in Education, 50*(3), 331–332.

Stovall, D. (2020). On knowing: Willingness, fugitivity, and abolition in precarious times. *Journal of Language & Literacy Education, 16*(1), 1–7.

United Negro College Fund. (2019, June 7). Retrieved from https://www.uncf.org/pages/k-12-disparity-facts-and-stats

Winn, M. T., & Behizadeh, N. (2011). The right to be literate: Literacy, education, and the school-to-prison pipeline. *Review of Research in Education, 35*, 147–173.

Wun, C. (2015). Against captivity: Black girls and school discipline policies in the afterlife of slavery. *Educational Policy, 30*(1), 1–26.

Woodson, C. G. (1933). *The mis-education of the Negro.* Trenton, NJ: Africa World Press.

2

THE *OTHER* TRAYVON

Anti-Black Racism and Violence against Black Lives

Meditation #3
Black love doesn't have to hurt.

On February 26, 2012, many people were numbed, hurt, and in pain at the murder of Trayvon Martin. It's still hard to believe that Trayvon's youth was taken away from him in just a matter of seconds by the hands of a man who viewed him as inhuman and by a society who saw his gray hoodie and his Black skin as threats. Trayvon's murder happened two days after my 23rd birthday. My soul remembers.

Trayvon Martin—a name that reminds me of the state-sanctioned racial violence that physically and symbolically abuses and kills the bodies, lives, and spirits of Black children and youth.

Trayvon Martin—a name that reminds me of the countless Black children and youth who fall prey to racial violence, especially since racial violence is deeply enmeshed within the American fabric.

Trayvon Martin—a name that reminds me that education can be utilized as a tool to shed light on the beauty of Blackness and affirm the humanity of Black youth.

Trayvon Martin—a name that reminds me that Black lives do matter, even in English language arts (ELA) classrooms and language and literacy education.

Trayvon Martin's unjust and horrendous death influences my journey and shapes who I am as a critical race English educator. To illustrate, it was Monday morning during my first year teaching. It was first period and students shared their celebrations. Each class period, I provided students with a communal and dialogic space to celebrate their small wins and victories and to highlight the things that were

DOI: 10.4324/9780429297052-3

going well in their lives. Right before the celebrations came to a close, a 15-year-old Black male student, ironically whose name was also Trayvon, raised his hand. I was surprised to see his hand in the air—we were six months in the game, and he had never celebrated with the entire class. He was a person who was quick to listen and slow to speak. However, instead of sharing a celebration with the class, Trayvon raised a question with me. He asked, "Mr. J, have you heard about the shooting of Trayvon Martin?" With a look of confusion, I replied, "No, I haven't." Trayvon, then proceeded to explain the story about Trayvon Martin's death and how that neighborhood watchman racially profiled and killed him.

As Trayvon continued to share the story about Trayvon Martin, a few students gave head nods of affirmation while echoes of, "*yeah, I heard about that*" permeated the room. Aaron, a Black male teenager, yelled, "Why did that watchman do him like that?" While I simultaneously facilitated the critical conversation, I also searched the web for a news media clip that would help explain the racial incident. In a space of contestation, I witnessed my 14- and 15-year-old Black students trouble and wrestle with the misperceptions, stereotypes, and racial violence that are inflicted upon Black lives. The students and I watched a CNN news report that attempted to explain the events that took place between Martin and the neighborhood watchman. After the clip ended, I asked a group of 14 Black boys and girls and 1 white female student the following questions: *What can we do to speak back and to speak up about the police brutality that transpires in communities? What is your definition of justice? Give an example of a time when justice was either served or not served in your own life or the life of someone you know.*

Should a person be able to defend him- or herself or themself if he, she, or they is in danger of being hurt or even killed? Should a person be able to use any weapon (including guns) to keep him or herself or themselves safe?

Do you feel that people of different races are treated equally in today's society? Give an example when you have experienced or seen unequal treatment. My soul remembers.

Trayvon Martin's ghost followed me that year. On July 13, 2013, George Zimmerman was found not guilty of the murder of Trayvon. I was angry, sad, and hurt. The death of Trayvon happened second semester, during my first year teaching; and, that summer, there was no justice for Trayvon. The death of Trayvon Martin showed me that "Black men and boys like Trayvon Martin had already been systemically criminalized, not by their individual actions but by their collective identity, their posture, their positionality, and sometimes even their fashion choices" (Ransby, 2018, p. 33). In the media and in school spaces, Black youth are positioned as violent and dangerous "bodies to be feared, contained, or even killed" (p. 33). That summer, as I critically reflected about my upcoming school year, I knew I could not enter my second year of teaching the way I entered the classroom during my first year.

Through the deconstruction and (re)construction of my ELA pedagogy and curricula, I had to create new curricula, lessons, and activities that focused on teaching in the wake of racial violence and teaching from a critical race English educator's perspective. I continued to center the language(s) and literacies of Black youth to counteract the hegemonic language and literacy practices that damage the souls of Black youth on a daily basis. My soul remembers.

After the murder of Trayvon Martin, President Obama exclaimed to the nation: "If I had a son, he would look like Trayvon." President Obama's powerful statement illuminates the shared racial, cultural, and gendered experiences between Martin and other Black boys. To this end, this chapter is about the *other* Trayvon. There isn't much distance between Trayvon Martin and the *other* Trayvon (Black children and youth) who sit in PreK–12 classrooms—who speak the same Black language and wear the same Black skin like Trayvon Martin and like Rekia Boyd, Laquan McDonald, Michael Brown, Renisha McBride, Jordan Edwards, Aiyana Stanley-Jones, Philando Castile, Alton Sterling, Oscar Grant, Malissa Williams, Timothy Russell, Tyre King, Jessica "Jessie" Hernandez, Jonathen Santellana, Anthony Nunez, Breonna Taylor, and countless more. These names represent not only Black males who tend to be the focus in conversations about the killing of Black people but also Black girls, women, and members of the LGBTQIA community whose bodies are also being abused, misused, and murdered by the hands of white supremacist patriarchy and police brutality. This chapter explores and provides insights about why these realities must matter in ELA classrooms.

#BlackLivesMatter in English Education and ELA Classrooms

The #BlackLivesMatter movement was initially created in direct response to the murder of Trayvon Martin and the acquittal of his killer, George Zimmerman. However, it also responds to a history of institutional, societal, and individual assault on Black lives nationally and globally. It is an action-oriented movement that unveils the operation of white supremacy and works to dismantle systems that have a deep history of state-sanctioned violence (Dumas & Ross, 2016; Rogers, 2018). #BlackLivesMatter was created by three Black queer women, Alicia Garza, Opal Tometi, and Patrisse Khan-Cullors (http://blacklivesmatter.com/about/).

According to the founders of the movement,

> When we say Black Lives Matter, we are broadening the conversation around state violence to include all of the ways in which Black people are intentionally left powerless at the hands of the state. We are talking about the ways in which Black lives are deprived of our basic human rights and dignity.
>
> *(Garza et al., 2021)*

The essence of the founders' argument is a response to the anti-Black racism that infiltrates our society and a call to action to challenge society to join the movement to dismantle all forms of Black oppression (i.e., race, gender, sexual orientation, class, nationality, and disability). Richardson and Ragland (2018) insist, "Black Lives Matter affirms the lives of Black queer and trans folks, disabled folks, black-undocumented folks, folks with records, women and all Black lives along the gender spectrum" (p. 29). It is important to realize that not only does #BlackLivesMatter focus on the physical violence that transpires against Black bodies, but it also delineates the symbolic violence that denies the humanity of Black people. One of the pivotal components of this movement is that it sheds light on honoring the humanity that resides within Black lives. In this light, #BlackLivesMatter hones in on the human aspect of mattering by rejecting dehumanization and anti-Black racism.

In these ways, the #BlackLivesMatter movement connects fundamentally to education, literacy, language, curriculum, and pedagogy. We see this in the responses of national educational professional associations. For example, the killings of Black youth have sparked much-needed conversations within the National Council of Teachers of English (NCTE), one of the foremost literacy education organizations globally. Scholar-activists within this organization are leading the way and, through their position statements, have challenged the field of English education and language and literacy studies to (re)consider how it is implicated in the tragic killings of Black people. In making this statement, the NCTE Black Caucus urges the field of English education to (re)imagine ELA curriculum as a revolutionized space that actively works against hegemonic language and literacy practices that oppress and wreak violence on the bodies of Black students in classrooms. In 2015, the NCTE Black Caucus released a statement that sheds light on the unjust murders of Black people and that affirms their humanity. The statement declares,

> In this light, we call upon English educators to use classrooms to help as opposed to harm, to transform our world and raise awareness of the crisis of racial injustice. We call upon English education researchers to commit time to studying and disrupting narratives of racism rendered complexly in the substance of our profession.

Similarly, the *Michigan Council of Teachers of English (MCTE)* released a statement (2020) that spoke back to the anti-Black racism and violence that have led to the deaths of Breonna Taylor, George Floyd, Ahmaud Arbery, Riah Milton, and Dominique "Rem' Mie" Fells. The Executive Committee of MCTE wrote that,

> As an organization of English educators, it is our responsibility to use literacy to work toward dismantling the systemic racism that leads to racial disparities in our communities and classrooms. Like communities and schools throughout this nation, the state of Michigan struggles with racist policies and practices that marginalize and harm BISOC (Black, Indigenous, Students of Color). This is evidenced by the Flint Water Crisis, an act of environmental racism and state violence that caused long-term health effects on Flint's children and their families after they were exposed to

lead poisoning when state officials switched their water supply. This is also evidenced by the Detroit Right to Literacy case where a group of Detroit students filed a lawsuit against the state of Michigan for a fundamental right to literacy (see *Gary B, et al. v. Whitmer, et al.*). Students should not have to fight for clean water, a basic right to literacy, or a right to live!

What I appreciate about MCTE's statement is that the document not only speaks to MCTE's role and responsibility to utilize language and literacy to dismantle anti-Black racism and violence but also the organization delineates how they have been complicit by tackling the ways in which MCTE upholds whiteness and white supremacy. For instance, they state, "Even so, we acknowledge that we have struggled with interrogating our organization's whiteness, and we have failed in being proactive and active in advocating for antiracism and equity and diversity within our organization, schools, and in public forums" (MCTE Statement, 2020).

In a 2015 issue of NCTE's *English Journal*, Groenke et al. (2015) ask the field of ELA to (re)imagine classrooms as spaces that disrupt whiteness and eurocentric conceptions of adolescents. The authors document their frustration with society's negative visions of Black adolescents and how these distorted visions lead to the "real" or emotional murder of Black youth. Within society's social imagination, Black adolescents are often viewed as "a menace to society," "thugs," and/or "sub-human." Groenke et al. state,

> The work of contemporary researchers focused on adolescence reminds us that those privileged in definitions of adolescence are also privileged in frameworks of education; those who are ignored in those definitions are also ignored in school. But who gets to be an adolescent and who doesn't? Whose adolescence matters in school and in life? Perhaps more importantly, who gets to live? Who gets to be human?
>
> *(p. 35)*

Groenke et al. (2015) ask educators to understand that we are *still* living in a time where Black people are viewed as inhuman, and encourage us to understand that in order to better serve Black students, the field of English education must reject racial violence within society and then recognize and dismantle it in classrooms. Failing to do so means that educators' complacency leads to English education being implicated in the perpetuation of racial violence.

Trayvon Martin's Death and the Dimensions of Anti-Black Violence in Schools

The death of Trayvon Martin links to the anti-Black violence that erupts within classrooms. Love (2013) explains how many teachers agree that George Zimmerman's actions were driven by racial profiling and anti-Black racism.

However, many of these teachers stop short of making connections to how the anti-Black racism and ideologies of Zimmerman are also reflected in their day-to-day living, curricula, teaching, and practices. These assumptions are tied to and reinforced by generations of white supremacist thinking which lead to educators' inability to identify anti-Blackness in their teaching and institutions. Trayvon's Black skin and Blackness made him a target and meant he was viewed as a criminal—not for his character or actions. Cooper (2017) explains, "Blackness always looks suspicious. Whiteness always looks safe" (p. 62). George Zimmerman reported to 911 that Martin appeared suspicious and "up to no good" (Hill, 2016). Time and again, these false narratives pertaining to Black males, Blackness, and Black people writ large are at the center of George Zimmerman's racist ideologies and beliefs which led to the death of Trayvon Martin (Love, 2013). Similarly, Black youth are racially profiled in schools because of generations of biases regarding intelligence, intent, and integrity as related to the color of their skin.

The anti-Black violence and racism that were displayed by George Zimmerman are developed by and rooted in the white imagination. Building upon the work of Mauldin and Johnson (forthcoming 2021), the white imagination is defined as "ideological thoughts and actions that are shaped around white logic, whiteness, patriarchy, and violence (i.e. physical, symbolic, linguistic, and curricular and pedagogical violence)." Ideologically, Zimmerman operated from the white imaginary which forced him to view Blackness as something to be feared and less than, which in return, is violent to Black people and our humanity. Author and poet Claudia Rankine exclaimed,

> When white men are shooting black people, some of it is malice and some an out-of-control image of blackness in their minds. Darren Wilson told the jury that he shot Michael Brown because he looked "like a demon." And I don't disbelieve it. Blackness in the white imagination has nothing to do with black people.
>
> *(Rankine, 2015)*

Time and again, these same negative claims and beliefs about Black youth seep into schools and push many teachers to fear, surveil, and police Black youth which, ultimately leads to the overrepresentation of Black youth in special education and high expulsion and suspension rates as opposed to their white counterparts. This is why we need Critical Race English Education. The white imagination lives and breathes in ELA classrooms, English education courses, language education, and literacy research that centers white and westernized language and literacy texts and practices that do not honor the lived experiences, knowledge production, and genius of Black people. The white imagination is the impetus for what Morrison (1992) calls the white literary imagination. In her book *Playing in the Dark: Whiteness and the Literary Imagination* (1992), Toni Morrison demonstrates how the white literary imagination produces white literary texts, literature, writing standards and theories, and language education that are overflowing with white ideologies and white supremacist patriarchy.

I want to call attention to the fact that the white literary canon protects and coddles white innocence and the white imagination. In novels such as *To Kill a Mockingbird, Huckleberry Finn, Lord of the Flies, The Great Gatsby, The Crucible, Fahrenheit 451,* and numerous more traditional (American) literary canonical texts, the writers embraced and embodied the white literary imagination, and they demonstrate and sustain their own ideological views of American exceptionalism (Gray, 2013). The white imagination and the white literary imagination have caused harm and damage to our Black youth outside in the streets and inside of schools. And it shows.

Baszile (2005) also argues that US schools serve as violent sites that oppress Black children and youth. She believes that the marginalization of Black youth is a criminal act committed by the hands of the US educational system in the name of "good education" through eurocratic (white-dominated) hegemonic policies and practices. With this notion of schools serving as violent sites, ELA teachers and literacy educators must understand that choosing eurocentric texts that omit the realities of Black people or misrepresent the multiple ways of being Black are actually forms of anti-Black racism and the devaluation of Black life. In like manner, educators have to consider the countless Black youth who experience racial fatigue, weariness, and spirit-murdering from sitting in classrooms where Black students are typically invisible (e.g., curriculum and pedagogy) yet hyper-visible (e.g., suspension, expulsion, and overrepresentation in special education classes). Educators must also consider pedagogies and practices that actively stand against the physical violence and other forms of anti-Black violence against Black lives (e.g., symbolic, linguistic, curricular, pedagogical, school, and systemic violence).

Michigan Teacher Accused of Assaulting Student Who Protested Pledge
by CHELSEA BAILEY

New Mexico police officer resigns after video shows him wrestling an 11-year-old girl to the ground 'because she took too much milk from the lunchroom'

Teacher Suspended After 6-Year-Old Black Boy Is Physically Assaulted at NY Charter School; Mother Searches for Answers

CLIFFSIDE PARK, N.J. – Students staged a walkout on Monday after a cellphone video appeared to show a New Jersey high school English teacher reprimanding three students for speaking Spanish and telling them to speak "American."

We cannot (re)imagine ELA classrooms as humanizing and radical spaces if we do not fully explicate the various ways ELA classrooms can often serve as violent sites. This is not to vilify ELA teachers but to illuminate how the dimensions of anti-Black violence and racism inform the educational experiences of Black youth (Johnson et al., 2019). This phenomenon of anti-Black violence is not anything new—it's historical and deeply etched within schools, classrooms, and society-writ-large: "Simply put, historically, Black people have encountered racial trauma and abusive acts in the name of so-called love in schools and in society since being in this country" (Johnson et al., 2019, p. 49). Johnson et al. describe five types of anti-Black violence that Black youth can encounter in schools (Figure 2.1): (1) *physical*—this form of abuse and assault stems from negative assumptions and racist ideologies; (2) *symbolic*—anti-Black violence that erupts from the misrepresentations of Black youths' racial and linguistic identities which leads to racial trauma and abuse of the spirit, soul, and humanity of Black people; (3) *linguistic*—this form of violence unfolds when Black youths' language is policed and negated through the privileging of white mainstream English; (4) *curricular/pedagogical*—this form of violence permeates schools' curricula through centering and teaching texts and standards that center white ways of living, speaking, and existing in the world; (5) *systemic*—systemic school violence is a form of violence in which schools' formations, language, processes, and policies mirror racist, sexist, classist, xenophobic, ableist, and homophobic ideologies.

Before Trayvon physically lost his life, he too was a Black youth who encountered the various types of anti-Black violence and racism described above. To illustrate, during the trial of George Zimmerman, defense attorney Mark O'Mara argued that the only reason George Zimmerman had been charged was because he is a white man. According to Hill (2016),

> Once it became clear that Zimmerman was White and Martin Black, he (O'Mara) argued, that fact alone served as a convenient way to see this story through a racial prism, to assert a racial agenda, and to refuse to recognize the incident for what it was: an act of self-defense. (p. 1821)

George Zimmerman's negative depiction and description of Trayvon Martin to the dispatcher show that he saw Martin as a threat. In addition, Mark O'Mara carried that same energy with him into the courtroom during the trial. The defense used Trayvon's school suspension (systemic violence) and alleged infractions the high school tried to inflict on Trayvon (symbolic violence); even though these alleged charges were dropped, O'Mara used Trayvon's harsh experiences with anti-Black violence in schools as part of his argument to paint Trayvon in a negative light to the jury. Similarly, Rachel Jeantel, a key witness in the case, was discounted on the stand by largely a white, monolingual jury who practiced anti-Black linguistic racism (linguistic violence) and discredited Rachel Jeantel, due to her use of Black Language and Creole English (Rickford & King, 2016). Let's be clear. This is why an anti-Black racial violence analysis is imperative: "Just because race cannot be isolated or proven in a court of law as a motivating factor does not mean it can be eliminated" (Hill, 2016, p. 1821). The many types of anti-Black violence that Black youth encounter must be recognized and worked against, especially when most ELA classrooms are filled with Black children and youth who share stories just like Trayvon's. Therefore, I stand and lean on the words of Love (2017) when she argues,

TABLE 2.1 The Dimensions of Anti-Black Violence in Urban Schools

Types of Violence	Definition	Examples
Physical	The physical abuse and assault that stem from racial discrimination and prejudicial ideologies and beliefs.	• Hitting, pushing, beating, etc. • Lynching • Police brutality • Sexual abuse • Sexual assault
Symbolic	A metaphorical representation of violence that stems from "racial abuse, pain, and suffering against the spirit and humanity of Black people" (author, under review).	• Racial epithets and slurs • Rejecting the experiences and lived realities of Black youth • Silencing the voices of Black youth • (Mis)reading Black youths' culture, race, gender, and language
Linguistic	This form of violence marginalizes and polices the language of Black youth (which is referred to as, e.g., Black Language, African American Language, or African American Vernacular English) through privileging and promoting white mainstream English.	• Socializing Black youth to view Black language as "not good," "broken English," and "incorrect" • Devaluing the connection between language, race, and identity • Teaching Black students and students from other ethnic groups that code-switching is the best approach to "master" white mainstream English (Baker-Bell, 2017[GB6]) • Teaching grammar and vocabulary in isolation from the texts we are teaching and disconnected from the lived realities and experiences of youth from racially and linguistically diverse backgrounds
Curricu-lar and peda-gogical	This form of violence infiltrates schools' curricula through teaching texts, materials, and standards that center eurocratic notions of existing and being in the world (Cridland-Hughes & King, 2015). In conjunction, the *conventional* curriculum provides a false narrative about Black people through promoting deficit-based ideologies which inform teachers' pedagogical and instructional practices in	• Enacting culturally irrelevant and unresponsive curricula • Selecting texts in which Black youth do not see characters who look like them reflected in dynamic and positive ways • Feeding Black youth inaccurate, distorted, diluted, incomplete, and sanitized versions of history • Presenting mathematicians and scientists who are predominately white, monolingual, and male while mathematicians and scientists who identify as women and people from linguistically and racially diverse backgrounds are omitted

(Continued)

TABLE 2.1 (Continued)

Types of Violence	Definition	Examples
	classrooms. In general, this is a form of epistemic violence which attacks Black ways of knowing.	• Omitting critical conversations from the curriculum that explore the intersections of race, gender, religion, language, sexuality, etc. • Unintentionally and/or intentionally minimizing how teacher positionality shapes curricular decisions and pedagogical practices.
Systemic school	This form of violence is deeply ingrained within schools' structures, processes, discourses, customs, policies, and laws which oftentimes reflect racist and hegemonic ideologies.	• Underfunded and overcrowded schools • Inexperienced teachers and/or teachers who are not certified in the subject area(s) they teach • Overrepresentation of Black youth in special education courses • Tracking • Disproportionality of Black youth in gifted and talented courses • Zero-tolerance school discipline policies • Lack of educational and support services that promote positive healthy development—physically, mentally, and emotionally

Adapted from Johnson et al. (2019).

"So long as educators continue to enforce policies that demonize innocent children, they thus allow for the murder of thousands of Trayvon Martins in classrooms every day" (p.15). In a similar spirit, I contend that if educators do not critique, analyze, and challenge their own production of anti-Black violence, then they have agreed to stand in the physical and spiritual death and dehumanization of Black lives.

In Orlando, FL, at Lucious and Emma Nixon Academy, a six-year-old Black girl was arrested and charged with battery for kicking a staff member (Chiu, 2019). The young Black girl's grandmother explained that the young girl's behavioral problem was a result of her sleep apnea, which is a medical condition. Although the battery charge was dismissed, the six-year-old was put in handcuffs, placed in the back of a police car, and taken to the juvenile detention facility where law enforcement fingerprinted her and took a mugshot. The physical violence and spirit-murder the young Black girl experienced are connected to the symbolic, linguistic, curriculum, pedagogical, and systemic violence that unfolds in many schools and classrooms. In another example, in Jersey Shore, PA, at Jersey Shore High School, a violent and racist video was posted on Facebook. In the video, a white male student chants, "I say nigger, you say nigger" (Brokaw, 2020) with other white students in the background responding to the call. This is an example of symbolic violence and how classrooms can be spaces that promote and engage in anti-Black violence and abuse of the humanity of Black lives. Not only are white youth engaging in symbolic violence through the use of racial epithets and slurs in classrooms but also white teachers have been sustaining symbolic violence through (mis)using and tossing around the N-word.

The word nigger is birthed from white supremacy, colonization, and anti-Black racism. Back in 2015, CNN did a segment titled *The N-Word in America: Who Can Say It? Who Decides?*—it's a shame we are still having this conversation about who can and cannot say the N-word. white people shouldn't use the word at all. Period. But I digress. During this segment, scholar-activist Marc Lamont Hill had to check radio talk show host, Ben Ferguson. Ferguson argued that the use of the N-word is divisive and, essentially, it is unethical and wrong that Black people can use the word and white people can't. Marc explained that "The N-word isn't divisive. white supremacy is divisive. Slavery was divisive. That's the problem. And maybe, it's not white people's position to tell Black people what to say" (CNN, March 17, 2015). To further illustrate this point, at Buchholz High School in Gainesville, FL, Robert Cecil, a ninth- and tenth-grade English language arts teacher, was recorded on camera arguing about the "accurate" usage of the N-word to his students (Woods, 2020). Cecil exclaims, "If you're black, you say nigga, but you don't say nigger." After outrage from the students, Cecil posed the following question to the class, "It's a free country, freedom of speech, right?" When teachers force students to engage in uncritical conversations about the N-word, they perpetuate symbolic and linguistic violence through dismissing the experiences of Black people and robbing students of learning about the sociohistorical, racial, cultural, and linguistic context of the word (Grinage, 2013).

In her brilliant and beautiful book, *Linguistic Justice: Black Language, Literacy, Identity, and Pedagogy*, Baker-Bell (2020) lets the people know that "whether we agree or disagree if the term is appropriate, most Black Language-speakers understand that nigga has a variety of meanings and has a different meaning from nigger" (p. 78). Nigger is a gut-wrenching reminder of a system that doesn't see Black people as human. That word is a violent remembrance of the enslavement of Black people across the African Diaspora and "a painful reminder of the atrocities that happened on plantations" (A. Rye, personal communication on Twitter, June 3, 2017). However, Black people have taken that word and changed the meaning and spellings; for Black people, it can signify homie, friend, associate, sista, brotha, lover, and partner (Baker-Bell, 2020). It is important to mention that even in Black communities the word nigga can be viewed as problematic, but "it has a different nuance from the racial epithet nigger" (Baker-Bell, 2020, p. 78). The (mis) reading of Black youths' culture, race, and language is not only symbolic violence but also linguistic violence. Undervaluing the intersection of language, race, and identity promotes white mainstream English as the only way to speak "correctly," denying Black Language as historic, structured, and literary, and centers whiteness, while other languages such as Black Language and Spanish are seen as less than and are often policed in classrooms (Baker-Bell, 2020; Martinez, 2017).

The multiple dimensions of anti-Black violence are not detached from one another and can operate simultaneously. For example, if teachers are inflicting linguistic and symbolic violence on the lives of youth who come from racially and linguistically diverse backgrounds through privileging white mainstream English, then, more than likely, those same teachers are also engaging in curriculum and pedagogical violence. As educators, our curricular choices and pedagogical practices are reflective of how we critically view and read the world; and when educators adhere to culturally irrelevant, white-dominant, and culturally unresponsive curricula, they are inadvertently employing a pedagogy of violence which has a lasting impact as all students develop "truths" about who and what counts. I am in agreement with Jones (2020) when she argues that,

> when we reserve the word violent as a descriptor for physical violence only, we fail to recognize the many ways in which non-physical injury happens, is normalized and, in the case of destructive pedagogy, harms students' learning and how they see themselves in it.

Curricular violence permeates classrooms through teaching texts, materials, and standards that center eurocentric perspectives and knowledge. To further illustrate this point, in Prentice Hall's textbook, *Literature: The American Experience* (Wiggins, 2010), a nationally adopted text in many high school ELA classrooms, the third unit, "A Nation Is Born," includes the speeches and literary works of Patrick Henry, Benjamin Franklin, Thomas Jefferson, and Thomas Paine. The voices of Black people during this particular time period are silenced. To complicate this erroneous notion of a growing nation grounded only in the work of white leaders, the textbook could have included the voices of prolific Black orators and poets. For example, David Walker's *Appeal to the Coloured Citizens of the World* (1729) is a political document that interrogates the authors of the Declaration by confronting the issues of racism, religion, and chattel slavery. Within this unit, there is one text by Phillis Wheatley, a Black female poet during the 18th century. However, it is important to understand that neither sprinkling the voices of Black writers throughout the textbook nor omitting Black people from the storylines disrupts the majoritarian narrative. This failure to disrupt the majoritarian narrative in the texts we choose is another example of how classrooms can sustain anti-Black racial violence and the spirit-murdering of Black students.

In their book, *Letting Go of Literary Whiteness: Antiracist Literature Instruction for White Students*, Borsheim-Black and Sarigianides (2019) call for the teaching of antiracist literature instruction and for the dismantling of whiteness in secondary English classrooms and within the fields of English education and language and literacy studies. The authors argue that,

Within the realm of English education, racism is woven into the fabric of traditional language, literacy, and literature curriculum, through the over-valuing of eurocentric grammar rules at the expense of African American language and the prioritization of White authors over literature represent-ing experiences of people of color.

(Borsheim-Black & Sarigianides, 2019, p. 6)

Within the world of literary studies and language and literacy studies, anti-Black racism and whiteness infiltrate the literature. In fact, the literary canon reflects the racist ideologies and white supremacist patriarchy that undergird the anti-Black racism that is propagated in society.

These levels of anti-Black violence and racism in and out of schools are the reasons I conceptualized Critical Race English Education. The background to Critical Race English Education is explained fully in the introduction to this book, but here I remind readers that it is a theoretical, curricular, and pedagogi-cal construct that tackles white supremacy, race, and anti-Black racism within the field of English education, ELA classrooms, and beyond. Uniquely, Critical Race English Education is a form of Black resistance that counteracts the violent prac-tices of education. The questions that undergird and guide my thinking about Critical Race English Education are: *(1) how are white supremacy and anti-Black racism re-inscribed through our disciplinary discourses and pedagogical practices?; (2) when we think about the curricula and pedagogical decisions and practices, whose identities are included and reflected in ELA curricular and pedagogies and how are our curricula and pedagogies inclusive of Black youth?; (3) how are we using Black youth life histories and experiences to inform our mindset, curriculum, and pedagogical practices in the classroom?* Racial violence is also the absence of who and what educators include in class-rooms. In the next chapter, I flesh out this framework more in-depth.

It is not a revelation that Black youth enter and exit ELA classrooms with racial wounds that stem from educators' onto-epistemologies saturated in west-ernized and euro-American ideologies and beliefs. These beliefs are the dominant and standard ideologies by which Black students are judged, which causes the racial wounds. Building upon this argument, in their special themed issue for the journal of *English Education* titled *From Racial Violence to Racial Justice: Praxis and Implications for English (Teacher) Education*, Baker-Bell et al. (2017) assert that our world is on fire and the students who are sitting in ELA classrooms are thirsty and in need of water. The authors write,

As coeditors of this issue, we think about what our society (on fire) and classrooms (thirsty) need. For us, both need to unlearn and engage in trans-formative conversations about anti-Blackness, homophobia, and other forms of xenophobia. To this, we offer what (Lamar) is calling *Critical Race English Education*, or *CREE* (as water).

(p. 123)

Critical Race English Education rings true to me because it allows ELA teachers and English educators to build revolutionary curricula, policies, and practices WITH Black youth so that the existence, resilience, struggle, triumphs, brilliance, and humanity of Black lives are honored.

Bibliography

Anderson, J. D. (1988). *The education of Blacks in the South, 1860–1935*. Chapel Hill, NC: The University of North Carolina Press.

Baszile, D. T. (2005). Criminal Acts in the name of good education. *Curriculum and Pedagogy, 2*(1), 20–23.

Baker-Bell, A., Butler, T., & Johnson, L. L. (2017). The pain and the wounds: A call for critical race English education in the wake of racial violence. *English Education, 49*(2), 116–129.

Baker-Bell, A. (2020). *Linguistic justice: Black language, literacy, identity, and pedagogy*. New York and London: Routledge.

Black Lives Matter. (2021, August 26). Retrieved October 7, 2021, from https://blacklivesmatter.com/

Borsheim-Black, C., & Sarigianides, S. T. (2019). *Letting go of literary whiteness: Antiracist literature instruction for white students*. New York: Teachers College Press.

Boutte, G. S. (2015). *Educating African American students: And how are the children?* New York: Routledge.

Brokaw, J. (2020, March 17). Online video of Jersey Shore students chanting racial slur under district investigation. *NorthCentral PA*. Retrieved from https://www.northcentralpa.com/education/online-video-of-jersey-shore-students-chanting-racial-slur-under/article_050bfe7c-5330-11ea-a231-d7efbcb0ef89.html

Chiu, A. (2019). Florida officer fired for 'traumatic' arrests of two 6-year-old students at school. Retrieved 17 March 2020, from https://www.washingtonpost.com/nation/2019/09/23/girl-tantrum-orlando-classroom-arrested-battery-school-investigation/

Chiu, A. (2020, March 17). Florida officer fired for 'traumatic' arrests of two 6-year-old students at school. Retrieved from https://www.washingtonpost.com/nation/2019/09/23/girl-tantrum-orlando-classroom-arrested-battery-school-investigation/

Cooper, B. C. (2017). Re-nigging on the promises: #Justice4Trayvon. In B. C. Cooper, S. M. Morris, & R. M. Boylorn (Eds.), *The crunk feminist collection* (pp. 59–64). New York: Feminist Press.

Cridland-Hughes, S. A., & King, L. J. (2015). Killing me softly: How violence comes from the curriculum we teach. In K. Fasching-Varner & N. D. Hartlep (Eds.), *The assault on communities of color* (pp. 67–71). Maryland: Rowman & Litttlefield Publishing.

Dumas, M. J., & Ross, K. M. (2016). "Be real Black for me": Imagining BlackCrit in education. *Urban Education, 51*(4), 415–442.

Foster, M. (1998). *Black teachers on teaching*. New York: The New Press.

Grinage, J. (2013). Combating Huck Finn's censorship: A step-by-step guide to discussing the n-word in the classroom. In S. Grineski, J. Landsman, & R. Simmons III (Eds.), *Talking about race: Alleviating the fear* (pp. 137–148). Sterling, VA: Stylus.

Groenke, S. L., Haddix, M., Glenn, W. J., Kirkland, D. E., Price-Dennis, D., & Coleman-King, C. (2015). Disrupting and dismantling the dominant vision of youth of Color. *English Journal, 104*(3), 35–40.

Hill, M. L. (2016). *Nobody: Casualties of America's war on the vulnerable, from Ferguson to Flint and beyond*. Atria Books.

Johnson, L. L. (2018). Where do we go from here?: Toward a critical race English education. *Research in the Teaching of English, 53*(2), 102–124.

Johnson, L. L., Bryan, N., & Boutte, G. (2019). Show us the love: Revolutionary teaching in (un)critical times. *Urban Review, 51*(1), 46–64.

Jones, S. P. (February, 2020). Ending curriculum violence. *Teaching Tolerance.* Retrieved from https://www.tolerance.org/magazine/spring-2020/ending-curriculum-violence

Kirkland, D. (2013). *A search past silence: Literacy, Black males, and the American dream deferred.* New York: Teachers College Press.

Ladson-Billings, G. (2014). Culturally relevant pedagogy 2.0: a.k.a the remix. *Harvard Educational Review, 84*(1), 74–84.

Love, B. L. (2013) "I see Trayvon Martin": What teachers can learn from the tragic death of a young Black male. *The Urban Review, 45*(3), 1–15.

Love, B. L. (2017). Difficult knowledge: When a Black feminist educator was too afraid to #SayHerName. *English Education, 49*(2), 192–208.

Love, B. L. (2019). *We want to do more than survive: Abolitionist teaching and the pursuit of educational freedom.* Boston, MA: Beacon Press.

Martinez, D. (2017). Imagining a language of solidarity for Black and Latinx youth in English language arts classrooms. *English Education, 49*(2), 179–196.

MCTE. (2020). MCTE'S commitments and action steps to move toward antiracism. Retrieved from https://mymcte.org/2020/06/04/mctes-commitments-and-action-steps-to-move-toward-antiracism/

Morrison, T. (1992) *Playing in the dark: whiteness and the literary imagination.* New York: Vintage Books.

NCTE. (2015). NCTE statement affirming #Blacklivesmatter. Retrieved from http://www.ncte.org/governance/pres-team_9-8-15

Paris, D. (2012). Culturally sustaining pedagogy: A needed change in stance, terminology, and practice. *Educational Researcher, 41*(3), 93–97.

Rankine, C. (2015, December 15). *Claudia Rankine: 'Blackness in the white imagination has nothing to do with black people'.* The Guardian. https://www.theguardian.com/books/2015/dec/27/claudia-rankine-poet-citizen-american-lyric-feature

Ransby, B. (2018). *Making All Black lives matter: Reimagining freedom in the 21st century.* Oakland, CA: University of California Press.

Richardson, E., & Ragland, A. (2018). #StayWoke: The language and literacies of the #BlackLivesMatter movement. *Community Literacy Journal, 12*(2), 27–56.

Rickford, J. R., & King, S. (2016). *Language and linguistics on trial: Hearing Rachel Jeantel (and other vernacular speakers) in the courtroom and beyond.* Presidential Address, Washington, DC, 7 January.

Rogers, R. (2018). *Reclaiming powerful literacies: New horizons for critical discourse analysis.* Routledge.

Winn, M. T. (2013). Toward a restorative English education. *Research in the Teaching of English, 48*(1), 126–136.

Woods, A. (2020). Racism in schools: Teachers using the n-word has become an uncontrollable classroom trend and the punishments are usually minimal. Retrieved 17 March 2020, from https://newsone.com/3903381/racism-schools-teachers-using-nword-become-uncontrollable-classroom-trend/

3

BLACK(NESS) IS, BLACK(NESS) AIN'T

Critical Race English Education

Meditation #4

Black is love. Black is beautiful. Black is joy. Black is fierce. Black is aggressive but Black is also peaceful. Black ain't evil. Black ain't torture. Black ain't soulless. Black is soul. Black is unapologetic. Black is free. Black ain't afraid. Black ain't monolithic.

Black is endless. Black is gentle. Black is complex—but Black is also simple.

Black is resilient. Black is strength. Black is vibrant. Black is opulent. Black is light but Black is also dark. Black is smooth. Black is delicate. Black is rough.

Black is off da chain. Black is dope. Black is magical. Black is limitless.

Black(ness) is _____.

Black(ness) is revolutionary. When I reflect on what it means to be Black, it prompts me to absorb what my Black(ness) is and what my Black(ness) AIN'T! On a daily basis, I meditate on Blackness and what it means to me. I cannot critically reflect and meditate on Blackness without acknowledging that love is at the center of Blackness. I'm reminded of the words from my good friend, Dr. ReAnna Roby, who eloquently exclaimed, "we can't have a revolution without love and we can't have love without Blackness" (personal communication, June 1, 2019). With that being said, I raise the following question: *What does it mean to love the hell out of Blackness, especially when we live in a world that misreads our Blackness, misrepresents our Blackness, and paints a negative image of our Blackness?*

Throughout the dark annals of history and in our current political and racialized context, Blackness is often positioned as "evil," "unintelligent," and "less than." This book tackles Blackness from multiple angles and perspectives while

DOI: 10.4324/9780429297052-4

challenging readers to think critically about the importance of reclaiming our heritage and knowledge as Black people across the African Diaspora. It is beyond the scope of this book, but it is noteworthy to mention that Blackness not only exists and applies to Black people within the United States, but also applies to Black people and Blackness across the globe. For example, Blackness and Black people are situated in different geographical contexts (e.g., Caribbean, Africa, Brazil, and Europe just to name a few). In order to understand Blackness in its entirety, we have to unpack Blackness across the African Diaspora and understand that Black people across the Diaspora connect to Africa. Blackness is clothed in that Motherland drip (Knowles, 2019). That is, to understand who we are as Black people, we have to understand how we were ethnic people before we were raced (Hilliard, 2009). Our stories as Black people across the African Diaspora do not start with the enslavement of Black people. We come from lineages of queens, kings, warriors, doctors, artists, mathematicians, scientists, and writers (Boutte, 2015). The Africanness connection to Blackness illustrates the resistance, resilience, and beauty that lie within Blackness (King, 2005).

Blackness is not monolithic. It is dynamic, fluid, and complex. Love (2019) contends that Blackness is more than skin hues and that Blackness has to be explored by taking into account the intersection of race, language, culture, gender, sexuality, dis/ability, religion, and spirituality. Blackness is women, girls, trans folks, boys, and men. Often neglected in conversations about Blackness, we can't be out here hollerin' about Black lives matter if we aren't considering the lives, experiences, and humanity of Black trans people. When exploring Blackness, our multiple identities are interconnected and cannot be discussed or explored in isolation of one another. Blackness is an embodied experience that is connected to Black people's culture, race, ethnicity, language, literacies, and ways of life. There is so much dopeness and beauty in Blackness.

In Solange Knowles' album, *A Seat at the Table*, her mom, Tina Knowles Lawson, offers an interlude that focuses on loving Blackness. Mama Tina explains, "I've always been proud to be Black / Never wanted to be nothing else, love everything about it." Building upon Mama Tina's sentiments, I'm deeply in love with my Blackness, and I unapologetically love on my Blackness. Overtime, I have come to understand that my Blackness is a description just as much as it is personal testament that connects to the political. I have come to know my selves on a deeper level because Blackness is a claim and commitment to who I am and to the folks who are in community with me. During a conversation with the homie, Dr. Dave Stovall, he explained that "Blackness is a title … but it is also a political understanding of your life in this place. It is an affirmation of what it is that you understand yourself to be and a willingness to fight" (personal communication, June 1, 2019).

According to Dumas and ross (2016), Blackness is an act of self-care, collective care, and resistance. As stated in the mediation above, my Black is off da chain. What I mean is that when I view my Blackness through the Black gaze, my Blackness is wild and free—not bound by the mental shackles and chains of whiteness. I am Black and off da chain because I do not view my Blackness through the white gaze. During a powerful conversation with my sista-schola, Dr. April Baker-Bell, we theorized and unpacked what it means when our Blackness is off da chain. She said a myriad of things that hit home for me but one point in particular is when she stated,

> This moment in my life I just don't give a fuck. I don't walk around in fear … I know and understand what is happening around me. By way of me knowing how white folks move, I understand it is not me with the problem. I'm free from whiteness judging me.

Dr. Baker-Bell's words are a whole entire mood and a half. This conversation left me feelin' energetic and not giving two cares about anybody's judgment of my Blackness and me.

Because Blackness has deep connections to Black people and communities, who have historically and currently been (mis)read by the media and within the literary canon, I utilize Critical Race English Education as a framework to challenge anti-Black racism and violence within language and literacy studies while also providing a justice-oriented framework that sheds love and light on the inherent beauty in Blackness. Unfortunately, the reality is that many Black youth are not given opportunities to explore positive aspects of Blackness, inspect their multiple identities, or the autonomy to engage with the racial justice movements of our current time such as #BlackLivesMatter and #SayHerName. Thus, Critical Race English Education serves as leverage to provide Black youth with humanizing curricula, pedagogies, and texts that assist Black students in constructing positive and transformative understandings of their racial, linguistic, cultural, and intellectual identities. The point here is not to argue that Critical Race English Education is the panacea for creating equitable and transformative classrooms nor am I arguing that Critical Race English Education can "save" Black youth—however, I do believe that if taken seriously, Critical Race English Education can serve as a breath of fresh air in an oppressive and dry environment.

The cultural memories of Black people have been and are still being obliterated and distorted as a part of ongoing cycles of oppression. Unfortunately, these pejorative and pathologizing views about Blackness permeate many ELA classrooms and school settings. Critical Race English Education is offered as a revolutionary and revitalizing framework, theory, curricula, and pedagogies that can assist in creating transformative and justice-oriented spaces for Black youth. In the age of standardized testing and accountability, many Black youth sit in ELA classrooms experiencing anti-Black violence and racism. Standardized testing continues to reflect a white, male, middle-class, and monolingual world; and, the identities, knowledge, and experiences of Black people are omitted. The curriculum and pedagogical violence Black youth often encounter in classrooms stem from teachers who serve a standardized curriculum (Baszile, 2009). There is a need to begin the healing process necessary for the reinstatement of Black peoples' humanity and worth. Healing will begin not only by telling more complete and truthful stories about history but also from critically engaging an array of Black voices in a space to wrestle with and tackle the politics around Blackness (King, 1991). Therefore, in ELA classrooms, we must begin to (re)define Blackness.

"You Don't Know a Thing about Our Story, Tell It Wrong All the Time"

In light of the current racial and political climate, language and literacy educators, ELA teachers, and literacy policymakers need to understand the relationship among literacy, anti-Blackness, violence, whiteness, freedom, and education. In her song titled "Baldwin," singer-songwriter-activist-storyteller Jamila Woods (2019) critiques US schools for their erasure of the Black experience through text selection that builds upon white history and standards. At the beginning of her song, she sings, "You don't know a thing about our story, tell it wrong all the time … Don't know a thing about our glory, wanna steal my baby's shine." The lyrics underline how our (Black peoples') cultural memories have been omitted and distorted through the use of white knowledge and perspectives about Blackness. whiteness is deeply enmeshed within the state-sanctioned ELA curriculum. Throughout history and even today, literacy has been racially and socially positioned as a right for white people and as a privilege for people of color, in this particular case, Black children and youth. On one hand, literacy has been used as a tool to further the oppression of Black people. There are past and current laws and policies that view literacy through deficit and scientific-based paradigms that infringe on the language and literacy practices Black youth bring into classrooms. During the enslavement of Black people, many states created anti-literacy laws and policies that prohibited Black people from reading and writing. If enslaved people were caught reading, writing, and/or spelling, they would encounter physical violence and punishment such as the losing of a body part, whippings, actual death, or sometimes being removed from their families through being sold to other enslavers.

Even through periods such as Reconstruction, Jim and Jane Crow, and the Civil Rights Movement, literacy was constructed as a violent tool to do harm to Black communities, specifically through utilizing literacy as a tool to suppress Black families and communities from voting and having a voice in the social, political, and economic workings of this country. However, in the midst of racial turmoil, Black children, youth, and adults have used literacy as a symbol of resistance and a means for freedom. The language and literacy practices of Black people were rooted in the multiple avenues they pursued to escape for freedom. They created songs such as "Follow the Drinking Gourd," "Wade in the Water," and "Go Down Moses" that were embedded with different clues and messages. To illustrate, "Follow the Drinking Gourd" provided coded messages and instructions on how to escape north for their freedom by following the North Star. Equally, spirituals such as "Wade in the Water" communicated that the best getaway route was along the river, and it signaled to enslaved Black folks, "to get off the trail and into the water so that the dogs used by enslavers could not pick up on their scent" (Baker-Bell, 2020, p. 70). Coded spirituals demonstrated how enslaved Black people utilized Black Language and Black literacies as ways to challenge, combat, and restore their humanity in the face of chattel slavery (Baker-Bell, 2020).

The language and literacy practices of Black people are also illuminated in our current context and insurgence of #BlackLivesMatter and #SayHerName. The chants, songs, art, and films of the current movements are embedded with rhetorical devices and moves that demonstrate how Black people use their own language and literacy practices as a means of resistance and for freedom. Richardson and Ragland (2018) explain the chants that #BlackLivesMatter activists employ are grounded in Black Language and literacy practices that are performed to resist white supremacy and anti-Black racism and affirm the humanity of Black lives. For example, in her article, Richardson explicates the chant "Babylon":

> Chant down Babylon
> > Black people are da bomb
> > We ready, we comin
> > We ready, we comin

Babylon represents the people and systemic structures that uphold whiteness and anti-Black racism and violence. Black Language is also threaded throughout the chant. For instance, Richardson states, "The chant describes Black people with the Black slang term *da bomb* that means 'superb, outstanding, excellent'" (as cited in Richardson, 2018, p. 33). We can also talk about how the use of "da" instead of "the" is reflective of Black Language. In Black Language, some consonants are dropped and some are replaced, for example, words such as comin'/coming, wif/with, ax/ask, and dey/they (see Baker-Bell, 2020). Black youth, historically and contemporarily, have demonstrated that literacy is not only something they have but also, it is a political and social act that they do (Kynard, 2013; Richardson & Ragland, 2018). Black youth have utilized their language and literacy practices to fight for access to be seen and heard throughout the curricula, instructional practices, and policies.

The aforementioned examples illustrate literacy as a racially contested facet that illuminates the nexus between literacy, anti-Blackness, violence, and education. We, as educators, cannot have critical conversations around language and literacy curricula, instructional practices, and policies without using a critical racial analysis, without understanding the complex ways in which anti-Blackness impacts language and literacy classrooms and policies, and without creating humanizing language and literacy experiences that can counteract the surveillance of Black youth. Racial justice-focused curricula should be embedded in and guided by Black people's cultural memories, histories, and literacies. The embeddedness and centeredness of Black knowledge, language, and literacies serve as rejection of anti-Blackness in ways that both interpret and resist ongoing cycles of oppression of Black folks, especially within schooling contexts.

Woodson (1933) illustrates how westernized and eurocentric-based curriculum often fail to include the knowledge, voices, and experiences of Black people. The stories and experiences of Black people are often distorted, incomplete, abbreviated, and omitted in school curriculum and spaces. In short, society-at-large will have to unlearn over 400 years of history in order to create a justice-oriented partnership between Blackness, Black people, and education. King (2005) states that, "first, truthful, equitable, and culturally appropriate education is understood to be a basic human right and not only as a condition of Black people's individual success and collective survival but is also fundamental to civilization and human freedom" (p. xxiii). This process allows for Black people to repossess our stories and (re)claim our cultural, racial, ethnic, and linguistic identities (King, 1991). Language and literacy studies and ELA classrooms have the potential to utilize language and literacy as tools to fight against racial, gender, and linguistic violence, oppression, and dehumanization. I now turn to the genealogy of Critical Race English Education and discuss how Critical Race English Education is inspired by and extends from critical race theory, BlackCrit, and critical literacy. That is, each of these theories contributes to the theorization of Critical Race English Education. It is worth mentioning that I'm not proposing that Critical Race English Education replaces CRT and BlackCrit. Instead, Critical Race English Education should be viewed as a member of the critical race family.

The Genealogy of Critical Race English Education

CRT and BlackCrit

Critical race theory (CRT) informs my research and teaching because, contrary to post- racial discourses, race *still* matters and racism is *still* alive and well. Decades ago, Ladson-Billings and Tate (1995) introduced CRT to the field of education. The authors argued that race was undertheorized in education; therefore, CRT would be an analytic tool to explicate race, racism, and white supremacy, and how these constructs contribute to the oppression of minoritized groups. In doing so, they also utilized CRT to examine curriculum, instruction, assessment, policy, and school funding (Ladson-Billings & Tate, 1995). Due to minoritized groups' personal encounters with racial oppression, Solórzano and Yosso (2002) emphasize that a key component of CRT is the centralization of the voices and lived experiences of people of color. This crucial dimension gives rise to the voices that are often unheard throughout US schools by allowing marginalized people to speak their pain and to tell their racialized and gendered stories.

Extending the conversation, Dumas and ross (2016) argue that CRT fails to explicitly address "the Black experience" and the racial oppression of Black people. That is, CRT does not adequately address anti-Black racism. BlackCrit is a response to CRT and other "crits"—specifically, LatCrit, AsianCrit, and TribalCrit, which have all developed as attempts to better identify and respond specifically to the racial oppression of Latinx, Asians and Pacific Islanders, and Indigenous groups (Brayboy, 2005; Chang, 1993; Hernandez-Truyol, 1997). Building on the tenets of CRT, Dumas and ross (2016) propose BlackCrit as a theory to better understand "the Black experience" and how anti-Black racism is located in laws, policies, and the everyday lives of Black people. BlackCrit in education can assist educators in understanding how social structures, policies, and practices are influenced by anti-Blackness. Jeffries (2014) states that anti-Blackness "is not merely about hating or penalizing Black people. It is about the debasement of Black humanity, utter indifference to Black suffering, and the denial of Black people's right to exist" (p. 1). Moreover, this anti-Black violence derives from anti-Black policies and practices, which continue the pain and suffering of Black children and youth in schools. Although CRT and BlackCrit are used in higher educational spaces and research (see Baszile, 2006; Bell, 1992; Stovall, 2015), CRT and BlackCrit as theoretical and action-oriented frameworks to understand race and anti-Black racism are underutilized in PreK–12 contexts.

Contributions of Black Women, Critical English Education, and Literacy Studies

There is a historical lineage of scholars who have called for racial justice work within ELA contexts. The work of Critical Race English Education builds on the foundational contributions and stands on the shoulders of Black women language and literacy scholars such as Geneva Smitherman, Arnetha Ball, and June Jordan, to name a few. Black women have always been at the forefront of many justice-oriented movements (e.g., slave uprisings, women's suffrage, the Black Arts Movement, the Black Freedom Movement, women's rights, the Civil Rights Movement, and LGBTQ movements). Historically and contemporarily, Black women continue to carry the torch of justice-oriented work. In a similar vein, I believe the social projects and epistemologies of Black women intellectuals provide robust frameworks for helping literacy studies understand the interconnection between language, race, identity, power, and pedagogy.

For example, Smitherman's (1979, 1995) body of work has historicized Black Language and literacies in relation to the Black Arts Movement and the BlackFreedom Movement. Black movements have shaped Black peoples' beliefs and imagination, and have "fundamentally reimagined and re-landscaped Black writing and reading" (Kynard, 2013, p. 127). Smitherman's work challenges past and existing theories that demonize Black youths' language and literacy practices while privileging white mainstream ways of speaking, reading, and writing.

During the late 1960s and 1970s, Smitherman (1979) understood that the ELA classroom had been engaging in fraudulent schemes against Black youths' linguistic repertoires. Smitherman (1995) asserts that

> the game plan has always been linguistic and cultural absorption of the Other into the dominant culture, and indoctrination of the outsiders into the existing value system (e.g., Sledd, 1972), to remake those on the margins in the image of the patriarch.
>
> *(p. 25)*

Her research demonstrated that through the ELA curriculum, schools reinforced racial and linguistic subjugation by protecting white norms and values.

Since then, language and literacy educators, composition studies scholars, and ELA teachers have been building on and adding to the conversation (see Baker-Bell, 2017; Kinloch, 2005; Kynard, 2013). This intergenerational dialogue is urgent, especially in a world that strives to erase the identities of Black girls and women (Butler, 2017). For example, Arnetha Ball and Ted Lardner (1997) theorize the interconnection between literacies, identity, and power through research on the preparation of teachers to work with youth who come from racially and linguistically diverse backgrounds. Ball and Lardner (1997) argue that teachers' uncritical and unconscious knowledge and attitudes about Black Language affect Black youths' learning experiences in writing classrooms. Given the racial and linguistic differences in language-use patterns and styles, many classroom teachers' negative attitudes toward Black Language develop from their lack of linguistic knowledge and utilization of narrow pedagogical techniques for teaching language skills (Ball & Lardner, 1997). Ball calls for writing teachers, literacy researchers, and ELA teachers to re-envision literacy and writing classrooms as transformative spaces that move toward more inclusive pedagogies that better support and sustain the oral and written literacies of Black youth.

The research of Geneva Smitherman and Arnetha Ball resonates with Caribbean poet, educator, and scholar June Jordan's 1982 keynote address to the National Council of Teachers of English, in which she queried, "What to do? What to do? ... English education acts as a gatekeeper ... closes down opportunities ... narrows rather than opens possibilities of social meaning and social action" (Stuckey, 1990, p. 97). In a time of racial chaos, when Black people are losing their lives at higher rates than any other racial and ethnic group as a result of state-sanctioned violence, white supremacy, and anti-Black racism, what is English education to do? Where do we go from here? Decades later, these questions continue to linger. As a counterhegemonic tool, Morrell (2005) proposes that the field increase its emphasis on critical English education in order to be "explicit about the role of language and literacy in conveying meaning and in promoting or disrupting existing power relations" (p. 313). Critical English education is intentional about the role social context plays in students' meaning-making practices. It also provides youth with the knowledge base to deconstruct canonical literature and popular culture texts such as media, art, and film, "while also instructing them in skills that allow them to create their own texts that can be used in the struggle for social justice" (Morrell, 2005, p. 313). Critical English education welcomes multiple languages, literacies, and modalities that are reflective of societal changes.

In conjunction with critical English education, I draw upon literacies studies scholars who are attentive to issues of race and identity (e.g., Kynard, 2013; Haddix, 2015). These frameworks view literacy as a political act that reflects one's racial, social, cultural, and geographical context. Furthermore, in contrast to prevalent skills-based approaches, these frameworks treat literacy as "something that people do, rather than something that they have or do not have" (Kynard, 2013, p. 32). Literacy studies has helped me to gain a better sense of how Black students have fought to be seen, heard, and humanized. I specifically draw upon critical orientations to literacy that refer to "the process of reading texts in an active, reflective manner in order to better understand power, inequality, and injustice in human relationships and contexts" (Boutte, 2015, p. 79). An essential element of critical literacy is Freire's (1970) notion that literacy is not only about reading the word but also about reading the world—societal events are texts that must be read, interrogated, and interrupted. Scholars such as Haddix (2015), Kirkland (2013), Paris (2010), and Sealey-Ruiz (2016) are all working at the intersections of English education and literacy studies, and have called for research and pedagogy to honor the literacies of Black youth and work to dismantle oppression.

What Is Critical Race English Education?

We need more complex racial frameworks that illuminate the beauty in Blackness and Black culture. Critical Race English Education is a theoretical and pedagogical framework that (a) challenges concerns such as anti-Black racism, whiteness, white supremacy, patriarchy, and violence that unfold in school contexts and outside-of-class spaces; (b) examines the historical and present-day relationship between literacy, language, race, and education by expanding the concept of literacies to include activist contexts and social movements such as slave rebellions, Reconstruction, Black Freedom Movement, Civil Rights Movement, #BlackLivesMatter, and #SayHerName, etc.; (c) aims to work against dominant and canonical texts that exclude the knowledge of Black people and the racial and ethnic experiences of Black people across the Diaspora; and (d) stands on the Black literacies that Black people have created over time and continue to form. Black literacies work against anti-Blackness because these literacies illustrate an unconditional love for Blackness and Black people.

Language and literacy educators cannot skirt around racial conversations around anti-Blackness and literacy. Although chattel slavery has been abolished in many places, the institution of slavery has been repackaged and infiltrates throughout our society. The institution of slavery has morphed in the sense that

Black communities (unknowingly or knowingly) still experience the remnants of its dehumanizing effects that linger within communities in outside-of-school spaces and within school contexts. From the over-surveillance and dehumanization of Black lives (i.e., the Flint Water Crisis, Dakota Access Pipeline, and the killing of unarmed Black youth) to the systemic policies and practices that limit and deny Black youth educational resources and to the lack of culturally relevant and culturally sustaining language and literacy practices, we must ask ourselves: how have the anti-literacy laws from the past evolved and how do they rest, explicitly/implicitly, within schools' and societies' current literacy initiatives? How can Critical Race English Education inform language and literacy curriculum? How can Critical Race English Education guide our current literacy policies and initiatives? What are the current literacy experiences for Black youth? How are literacy educators, ELA teachers, school administrators, and policymakers creating new language and literacy policies and curricula to sustain and support the language and literacy practices and experiences of Black youth?

The questions above show the political nature of literacy, the denial of literacy to Black students, and the possibility of creating and reimagining language and literacy curriculum and policies where Blackness and Black voices are at the center. The anti-literacy laws from the past have been altered but still show up and enter the doors of schools and ELA classrooms in the present. Take, for example, the landmark ruling that children have a constitutional right to literacy. In 2016, a group of Black and Brown students from Detroit filed a lawsuit against the state of Michigan, claiming the state was in violation of the 14th amendment. The students argued that the state had violated and deprived them of their rights to literacy through creating toxic spaces such as dilapidated school buildings, outdated textbooks, and large teacher shortages. These toxic conditions impacted the decisions and teaching of the students.

As a result, some of the students have spoken out about the difficult challenges they have faced with participating in society (Goldstein, 2020). As a scheme to deny political and economic power, the history of education shows us that anti-Black racism has created societal structures that withhold education and literacy from Black people. The students and their families recognized the educational system had purposefully failed them and was never intended to work in their favor. They freedom dreamed and fought to dismantle and replace anti-literacy practices with more humanizing literacy practices. The group of students believed that a more radical way of teaching literacy could be created. In May 2020, the state of Michigan reached a settlement. Funds were allocated for literacy initiatives and efforts, reduction in class sizes, professional development for teachers, one-to-one technology, and anti-racist curriculum and pedagogies. In the words of Jamarria Hall, one of the students and plaintiff in the lawsuit, "The fight is not done yet. We were fighting just to get into the ring. Now we're in the ring. Now the fight really starts." Despite the fact that a settlement was reached, the students and families know this is just the beginning and still have a long way to go.

Diminishing Black youths' lived experiences through upholding white language and literacy practices will not shape ELA classrooms in transformative ways. In no way am I arguing that the field of language and literacy is "bad"; however, it isn't completely "nice." Language and literacy studies and ELA classrooms are not exempted from the racial, linguistic, and gender inequities that unfold in society and within schools. Consequently, this calls for more complex racial frameworks within the field of language and literacy studies and English education that explore the historical antecedents of literacy and anti-Blackness that connect to the present-day injustices surrounding literacy. Critical Race English Education can be extrapolated not only to ELA classrooms but also can be situated within school leadership, literacy policies, and initiatives. Literacy does not only belong to ELA teachers—school administrators and policymakers must begin to understand the racial complexity that rests within literacy and why it is important for school leaders and policymakers to be in conversation with ELA teachers and literacy educators about what critical literacy frameworks such as Critical Race English Education would look like when applied on a classroom, school-wide, and policy level.

Don't Get It Twisted ... Critical Race English Education Is for You Too

School Leaders and Administrators

Literacy educators and ELA teachers cannot lead youth in critical dialogue and transformative pedagogical practices about the intersections of anti-Blackness, literacy, language, and education alone. It will also require key players such as school leaders and administrators (i.e., principals, assistant principals, curriculum coordinators, guidance counselors, and literacy specialists/coaches) to expand their conceptualizations of literacy and to view each educator in the school as a teacher of literacy. Though I concede that Critical Race English Education is concentrated in English education, I still insist it expands beyond ELA classrooms. Literacy is more than reading what is in print—it is also about reading what is not seen. Literacy reflects our racial, geographical, cultural, linguistic, and political identities and contexts. School leaders and administrators need to understand that ELA teachers and literacy coaches are not the only faculty in schools who are responsible for being teachers of literacy, because I believe we are all teachers of literacy. Reading, writing, speaking, thinking, and listening skills are not only confined to ELA classrooms. Students are required to engage in written and oral modes of communication in math, science, social studies, art, and music. It is beyond the scope of this book, but national and state standards for other disciplines have been adamant about creating explicit literacy-focused standards and curricula (see International Reading Association Standards for Middle and High School Literacy Coaches, 2006).

To be clear, many PreK–12 schools have school-wide literacy initiatives; however, these school-wide literacy policies and initiatives are often grounded in sanitized notions of literacy. The ELA and literacy curriculum that educators have to implement is typically mandated by the principal and/or the curriculum specialist, and because of this, school leaders have to possess deep content and pedagogical knowledge about literacy, language, critical race frameworks, and critical racial consciousness. School leaders and administrators are instructional drivers of the school. They plan and design curricula, oversee instructional practices, preside over professional development, and supervise extracurricular activities. If school leaders consider implementing Critical Race English Education on a school-wide level, it will begin to engage faculty and staff in notions of literacy, anti-Blackness, community, education, and racial justice. Having an extensive understanding of Critical Race English Education is instrumental for school leaders because it can help school leaders to assist teachers on how to re-envision and build curricula and pedagogical practices that create justice-oriented spaces. If school leaders do not create spaces for educators to engage in critical race conversations and practices or expand educators' knowledge base about what literacy is and how literacy is racially contested, whiteness remains unchecked and continues to underscore how schools operate because race is not at the forefront. Due to the fact that many teachers do not take race into consideration, Critical Race English Education has the potential to build educators' racial consciousness. It provides school leaders with a framework that dismantles anti-Black racism, honors Blackness, and creates more racially just schools.

Language and Literacy Policymakers

Educators cannot have conversations about (re)constructing ELA and literacy curricula, instructional practices, and initiatives without having literacy policymakers at the table. This is important because policy is interconnected to the curriculum and day-to-day instruction that takes place in classrooms. Many of the past and current literacy initiatives and reading programs that permeate school spaces are usually grounded in linear and traditional views about literacy which focus on fluency, names and sounds of letters, active comprehension, decoding of words, and vocabulary. These myopic literacy policies often do not include the knowledge and voices of Black people, Black literacies and language practices, or Black justice-oriented movements. Concomitantly, literacy policies and initiatives that are mandated throughout schools are not considering the anti-Black violence and struggle of youth in outside-of-school spaces and how this violence is linked to the anti-Black violence that happens within school contexts.

While current research takes a keen look at anti-Blackness, race, violence literacy, language, writing, and education, particularly within university settings and P–12 classrooms, these cutting-edge language and literacy theories and scholarship are still undertheorized and lacking within the policy world and conversations.

How can we effectively use language and literacy research to shape educational policy and the language and literacy experiences of Black youth? We can begin by channeling the spirits of our language and literary elders and leaders. Black Language and literacy scholars have been explaining that we need to build liberating and humanizing language and literacy policy for decades. As language and literacy scholars, ELA teachers, school leaders, and literacy policymakers, we must ask how our policies can reflect more inclusive ELA curricula that center the Black experience, Black Language, and Black literacies and the language and literacy practices of Black children and youth.

In closing, I suggest the following justice-oriented recommendations using the foundations of Critical Race English Education as a basis:

- It is time for a language and literacy policy and curricular shake up. The current language and literacy policies need to be dismantled and made anew. We have to (re)imagine language and literacy curriculum and policy that aim to humanize as opposed to harm the lives of Black youth. The language and literacy policies that drive classroom curriculum and instruction should reflect the lived experiences and knowledge of Black people. Also, it is important to note that when we center Blackness, we aren't excluding the voices and experiences of other groups of color (i.e., Indigenous, Asian Pacific Islander, and Latinx). Blackness is dynamic and fluid not static—to show the complexity of Blackness, we have to illustrate Black communities' relationships with other communities of color.

- Language and literacy scholars, ELA teachers, school leaders, and policymakers need to build bidirectional relationships among each other. Research and practice intersect—thus, ELA classrooms and schools-writ-large need humanizing research that centers Blackness in a non-deficit manner while uplifting the language and literacies of Black people. This cutting-edge research can drive our curricular decisions and pedagogical strategies. Similarly, having language and literacy researchers who explore the intersections of anti-Blackness, literacy, language, and education at the table with school leaders, ELA teachers, and policymakers can help illustrate the many ways the past and present-day ELA and literacy curriculum and pedagogy sustain whiteness and anti-Black racism and marginalize the voices and life histories of Black youth.

- The current language and literacy curricula, policies, and initiatives should be racial justice-focused. It is crucial that we begin to move beyond "social justice"-focused ELA curriculum because even within a social justice framework issues of anti-Black racism, violence, whiteness, and white supremacy go unmarked and unchecked. Racial justice-centered curricula and policies intentionally shift ELA classrooms to engage in critical race frameworks and pedagogies, in this case Critical Race English Education. This is showcased through our selection of texts and stories that we teach in ELA classrooms, our instructional strategies, and, most importantly, racial justice should be illustrated through our dispositions, and beliefs.

References

Baker-Bell, A. (2017). For Loretta: A Black woman literacy scholar's journey to prioritizing self-preservation and Black feminist- womanist storytelling. *Journal of Literacy Research, 49*, 526–543.

Baker-Bell, A. (2020). *Linguistic justice: Black language, literacy, identity, and pedagogy.* New York and London: Routledge.

Ball, A., & Lardner, T. (1997, March 13). *Dispositions toward literacy: Constructs of teachers knowledge and the Ann Arbor English Case.* Conference on College Composition and Communication, Phoenix, AZ, https://www.researchgate.net/publication/264840009_ Dispositions_Toward_Literacy_Constructs_of_Teacher_Knowledge_and_the_Ann_ Arbor_Black_English_Case

Baszile, D. T. (2006). Rage in the interest of Black self: Curriculum theorizing as dangerous knowledge. *Journal of Curriculum Theorizing, 22*(1), 89–98.

Baszile, D. T. (2009). "Deal with it we must: Education, social justice and the curriculum of hip hop culture." *Equity and Excellence, 42*(1), 6–19.

Bell, D. (1992). *Faces at the bottom of the well.* New York: Basic Books.

Boutte, G. S. (2015). *Educating African American students: And how are the children?* New York: Routledge.

Brayboy, B. M. J. (2005). Toward a tribal critical race theory in higher education. Paper presented at the meeting of the Association for the Study of Higher Education, Richmond, VA.

Butler, T. T. (2017). "#Say[ing] HerName as critical demand: English Education in the age of erasure". *English Education, 49*, 153–178.

Chang, R. S. (1993). Toward an Asian American legal scholarship: Critical race theory, post-structuralism, and narrative space. *California Law Review, 81*, 1241–1323.

Dumas, M. J., & Ross, K. M. (2016). "Be real Black for me": Imagining BlackCrit in education. *Urban Education, 51*, 415–442.

Freire, P. (1970). *Pedagogy of the oppressed.* New York: Continuum International Publishing.

Goldstein, D. (2020, April 27). Detroit students have a constitutional right to literacy, court rules. Retrieved from https://www.nytimes.com/2020/04/27/us/detroit-literacy-lawsuit-schools.html

Haddix, M. (2015). *Cultivating racial and linguistic diversity in literacy teacher education: Teachers like me.* Routledge and National Council of Teachers of English.

Hernandez-Truyol, B. E. (1997). Indivisible identities: Culture clashes, confused constructs, and reality checks. *Harvard Latino Law Review, 2*, 199–230.

Hilliard, A. G. (2009). What do we need to know now? In W. Au (Ed.), *Rethinking multicultural education: Teaching for racial and cultural justice* (pp. 21–36). Milwaukee, WS: Rethinking Schools, Ltd.

International Literacy Association. *Standards.* Retrieved August 15, 2020, from https://www.literacyworldwide.org/docs/default-source/resource-documents/standards-for-middle-and-high-school-literacy-coaches.pdf?sfvrsn=5264a28e_4

King, J. E. (1991). Dysconscious racism: Ideology, identity, and the miseducation of teachers. *The Journal of Negro Education, 60*, 133–146.

King, J. (2005). *Black education: A transformative research and action agenda for the new century*. New York: Routledge.

Kinloch, V. F. (2005). Revisiting the promise of students' right to their own language: Pedagogical strategies. *CCC, 57*(1), 83–113.

Kirkland, D. (2013). *A search past silence: Literacy, Black males, and the American dream deferred*. New York: Teachers College Press.

Knowles-Carter, B. (2019). So much damn swag interlude. In *Homecoming: The Live Album*. New York, NY: Parkwood Entertainment.

Kynard, C. (2013). *Vernacular insurrections*. Albany, NY: State University of New York Press.

Jeffries, M. (2014, November 28). Ferguson must force us to face anti-blackness. Retrieved from https://www.bostonglobe.com/opinion/2014/11/28/ferguson-must-force-face-anti-blackness/pKVMpGxwUYpMDyHRWPln2M/story.html

Ladson-Billings, G., & Tate, W. F. (1995). Toward a critical race theory of education. *Teachers College Record, 97*, 47–68.

Love, B. L. (2019). *We want to do more than survive: Abolitionist teaching and the pursuit of educational freedom*. Boston, MA: Beacon Press.

Morrell, E. (2005). Critical English education. *English Education, 37*, 312–321.

Paris, D. (2010). 'A friend who understand fully': Notes on humanizing research in a multiethnic youth community. *International Journal of Qualitative Studies in Education, 24*(2), 137–149.

Richardson, E., & Ragland, A. (2018). #StayWoke: The language and literacies of the #BlackLivesMatter movement. *Community Literacy Journal, 12*(2), 27–56.

Sealey-Ruiz, Y. (2016). Why Black girls' literacies matter: New literacies for a new era. *English Education, 48*(4), 290–298.

Smitherman, G. (1979). Toward educational linguistics for the first world. *College English, 41*(2), 202–211.

Smitherman, G. (1995). Students' right to their own language: A retrospective. *English Journal, 84*(1), 21–27.

Sledd, J. H. (1972). Bi-dialectalism: The linguistics of white supremacy. *English Journal, 58*(9), 1307–1315.

Solórzano, D. G., & Yosso, T. J. (2002). Critical race methodology: Counter-storytelling as an analytical framework for education research. *Qualitative Inquiry, 8*, 23–44.

Stovall, D. O. (2015). Normalizing Black death: Michael Brown, Marissa Alexander, Dred Scott, and the apartheid state. In K. Fasching-Varner & N. D. Hartlep (Eds.), *The assault on communities of color* (pp. 67–71). Lanham, MD: Rowman & Littlefield.

Stuckey, J. E. (1990). *The violence of literacy*. Maryland: Rowman & Littlefield Publishing.

Woods, J. (2019). Baldwin. In *LEGACY! LEGACY!* Chicago, IL: Jagjaguwar.

Woodson, C. G. (1933/1990). *The mis-education of the Negro*. Trenton, NJ: Africa World Press.

LOVE LETTER II

Michael Brown AKA "Big Mike"

Michael,

Writing this love letter has been difficult. It is sad and disheartening that I write to you under these circumstances. When I heard about what happened to you, I was devastated. Over time, I have gained an understanding of who you were before you became Michael Brown the 18-year-old teenager who was killed by a white male police officer. I wanted to learn more about Michael Brown—AKA Big Mike—AKA The Dreamer.

In many ways, you and I are different, but also we share many similarities. Like me, you had aspirations and goals that you were working to manifest. You had a passion for education, and you were preparing to start college. I was hyped when I read that your favorite movies were *House Party* and *Scary Movie II*. Lol. They are classics. *House Party* will never get old, especially that iconic dance scene where the famous Kid 'N' Play dance was birthed, as Full Force Smoove's song, "Ain't My Type of Hype," bumped and blasted in the background. Like me, music has a special place in your heart. Your family and friends raved about how you wanted to become a famous rapper and that your rap name is Big Mike. I don't wish to become a rapper, but I like to write music … I love to write R&B, rap, and trap lyrics. I'm not the best freestyler; I concentrate too hard on what I want to say instead of being relaxed and just letting it flow. However, if you give me a few hours, days, weeks, or even months, I can create some bars.

Speaking of bars, I checked out your Soundcloud page. Listening to the songs you created brought me an abundance of joy. Hearing your voice gave me chills and grabbed my heart. Also, while listening to a few of your songs, I laughed out loud. During an interview, your mom and grandmother mentioned that you were a silly and goofy person. From observing your SoundCloud, you posted content frequently which demonstrates your tenacity and hustle and your drive to follow

DOI: 10.4324/9780429297052-5

your dream. When I listen to your music, I hear remnants of trap-rap artists. For example, in some of your beats and lyrics, I hear the lyrical influence of Gucci Mane. A few weeks ago, Gucci Mane and Jeezy did an epic Verzuz battle. Verzuz is created by Timbaland and Swizz Beatz. Verzuz grew out of the need for Black joy during a global pandemic that has impacted the Black community. The beauty in Verzuz is that it (re)imagines what hip hop battles can look, feel, and sound like. Two notable and talented producers, singers, rappers, or songwriters connect live on Instagram and compete to see who has the better music catalog. The Verzuz battles are 100% Black; and I luv it. Digitally, Verzuz brings millions of Black people together to celebrate and love on Blackness, Black people, Black music, Black artists and entertainers. We've seen Patti LaBelle vs. Gladys Knight, Brandy vs. Monica, Lil John vs. T Pain, and 2Chainz vs. Rick Ross just to name a few. Two things I love about the Verzuz battles are the live commentary during the performances and the memes and gifs that Black folks have generated, which are absolutely hilarious. The live commentary and the creation of memes and gifs are constant reminders of the ingenuity, creativeness, wit, and imagination that Black people possess.

The Verzuz battles are for the culture. What I have found beautiful about some of the battles is that they have (re)connected Black artists and entertainers who have or had beef. Millions of Black people across the world watched R&B singers, Monica and Brandy, love on each other in love-affirming ways. Similarly, millions of people tuned in to catch the Jeezy vs. Gucci battle; I felt like I was watching a professional boxing match. I'm sure you know about the Gucci vs. Jeezy beef which lasted for about 15 years. After a night of tension and verbal clapbacks, in the end, we watched two Black men work through their past issues in order to move forward in the present, especially when the world is on fire and we constantly witness the ongoing war and assault against Black life. Verzuz is a healing space. As Black men, we have to understand Black masculinity. We must be critically reflective and conscious of the ways in which society constructs Black males and how we are susceptible to toxic masculinity, patriarchy, and white supremacy. Although Jeezy and Gucci's relationship has a long way to go, the world witnessed them demonstrate vulnerability and we watched them put their egos to the side.

Jeezy explained that he and Gucci needed to squash and settle their beef because it is bigger than the both of them and that Black lives are being feared, surveilled, and policed, due to a system that was designed to never love us. In addition, Jeezy expounded on how imperative it was for he and Gucci to unite because when we (as Black people) are strongly connected and unified, Black people are unstoppable and can't be touched. As I reflect on the Gucci and Jeezy Verzuz battle, I'm reminded of one of your songs, "SMH." In the song, you state, "Devil get off my back / I'll knock you off your feet / Another man down in my city." Whew … Big Mike, this is a whole entire word. These powerful words connect to Jeezy's response to Gucci and your dynamic words connect to an article that Dr. David Stovall wrote back in 2013. The title of the piece is "'Fightin' the Devil 24/7': Context, Community, and Critical Race Praxis in Education." Stovall argues that living in a world that feeds off anti-Black racism and violence, inequitable education, gender violence, unfair housing and healthcare, and mass incarceration is the reality for many Black folks and that it is like "fightin the devil 24/7." In this case, the evil incarnate, the devil, is anti-Black racism and white supremacy. Stovall (2013) states that "'the devil' speaks to the forces at play that work to prevent historically underrepresented, under-resourced, and disinvested groups or communities from attaining equitable, quality education" (p. 290). Although Dr. Stovall is focusing on community-centered education, you both point out that the "devil" stay busy in classrooms and in the streets.

In closing, writing this love letter has pushed me to think more about the ways we can work to humanize people who were murdered by the hands of state-sanctioned violence. I hate we even have to do this. Recently, while on Facetime with one of my best friends, Shel Lessington, she and I had a powerful conversation. I explained some of the amazing and dope things I have learned about you. She eloquently reminded me that you were already telling, writing, and creating your story. Through listening to your music, I was able to reclaim your history and connect it with the present and future. Thank you for your music, knowledge, and brilliance. Long live Big Mike.

Love,
LLJ

4

DOIN' IT WRONG

Rethinking Reading and Writing Workshop

Meditation #5
When you live and embody the Black radical imagination, you don't wait for them to create a seat for you at their table. You don't even worry about wanting to strategize ways to sit at their table. Because when we live within the Black radical imagination, we have created and still are creating our own shit.

It was the summer of 2011—I had just finished graduate school with my master's in secondary teacher education. Like most people who are preparing to enter their first year of teaching, I was hyped and nervous about having my own class-room, but I still looked forward to meeting my students. It was a Tuesday morning. I was on my way to my new school, Timberwood High School, to meet with my co-department chairs—Tiffany Smith and Dr. Mark Peterson (pseudonyms)—to receive the keys to my classroom and to receive my curriculum and book list for the upcoming school year. Drake's *Take Care* album blasted loudly from the speak-ers of my 2009 Grey G6 Pontiac. That album still rides—it's a classic. For those who do not know, Drake is a rapper, singer, songwriter, creator, and producer. Before becoming *Drake, the artist*, he was Jimmy, a basketball star, on the teen drama series *Degrassi: The Next Generation*.

Drake is the artist who many people love to hate—people say that he stays in his feelings. Maybe, there is some truth to that statement, but I have discovered there is a place for those feelings in the classroom. Once I created a unit titled *Teenage Love Affair*—*Romeo and Juliet* was one of the companion texts of study. The theme of ill-fated love allowed me to incorporate art work, music, nonfiction, and fiction texts that centered on this notion of love. I used Drake's song, "Find Your Love," to put into conversation with Shakespeare and to teach and illustrate

DOI: 10.4324/9780429297052-6

Drake's utilization of literary devices and elements and storytelling. Drake's rhythmic flow is impeccable and his ability to use literary devices and rhetorical moves to tell his stories illustrates that many rappers and singers are authors, writers, and storytellers and their stories and texts should be recognized for their literary merit and value and incorporated into the ELA curriculum.

The traditional ELA curriculum does not honor and acknowledge the lived experiences and stories of Black people and it displays Blackness in a negative light. Teaching a curriculum shaped by hip hop countered the mandated school curriculum that was provided to me (Baszile, 2009). Hip hop is more than rapping and dancing; it is resistance and a social movement that responds to, critiques, and challenges racial, class, and gender discrimination and oppression (Love, 2019). I did not utilize hip hop as a mnemonic device to assist in students' retention of information. I incorporated hip hop in my classroom as a way to illustrate self-expression, political resistance, social oppression, Blackness, love, and freedom.

As I pulled into the school's parking lot, my heart began to beat fast with excitement. While walking through the hallways, I was met with the clutter of desks, bookshelves, file cabinets, and carts filled with computer monitors and hard drives. Although I had not received my curriculum guides and my official classroom space, I knew I would be teaching mostly freshmen which meant my classroom would be somewhere on A-Hall. Tiffany and Dr. Peterson only taught upperclassmen, so their classes were on E-Hall, which felt like miles away from A-Hall. Trust me, that walk was no joke. When I reached the threshold of E-Hall, I could see Tiffany and Dr. Peterson. Tiffany was about 5′3″ or 5′4″. She was wearing a bright orange shirt with a white silhouette of a tiger, which was the mascot of her undergraduate alma mater, Clemson University. Clemson University is a flagship university in the southeastern region of the United States located in South Carolina. Tiffany's dark blue denim shorts accompanied her beaming orange shirt. She wore a dark, plum purple lipstick. I later discovered that the plum lipstick was Tiffany's favorite because she wore it pretty frequently. Tiffany's hair was midnight black and her shiny, dark curls touched her shoulders. Her hair was styled in a wrap. I can't remember exactly what Dr. Peterson wore that day, but I know it was a collared Ralph Lauren Polo tucked in his light blue denim jeans. I remember having a conversation about his collared polo because I, too, was wearing one, but I was rockin' a different color. Dr. Peterson had a grayish and blonde goatee; and, he always carried a friendly smile with him.

Tiffany and Dr. Peterson greeted me with pleasant and welcoming smiles and hellos. We met in Tiffany's classroom which was adjacent to Dr. Peterson's class. Although they were co-chairs, Dr. Peterson was retiring at the end of school year. Tiffany was going into her 17th year as a secondary ELA teacher. Dr. Peterson was in his 30th year of teaching secondary ELA; he also taught college literature and writing courses as an adjunct professor at local universities. Tiffany and Dr. Peterson presented me with the English department's curriculum for 9th–12th grade. They gave me the teacher editions to the textbooks I was "mandated" to use. Let me just say that Tiffany and Dr. Peterson were ecstatic about the curriculum and where the department was as a whole. In the meantime, I was in a deep pensive mood while trying to fake a smile. I was disturbed by the selected required texts and that the curriculum had not been updated since 2002. It was now 2011 and the curriculum had not been updated or revised.

I was frustrated to see novels such as *The Great Gatsby, The Crucible, Of Mice and Men*, and *The Scarlet Letter* as well as poets such as Thoreau, Whitman, Emerson, Dickinson, Poe, and Eliot, just to name a few (Figure 4.1). The same white men and women I encountered during my high school years and during my undergraduate studies at a flagship PWI in South Carolina. Although I was frustrated, I wasn't surprised. Timberwood High School was a unique space—1,400 students attended the school. Black students made up 68% of the school's student population. But, of course, the teachers were predominately white, and clearly, the curriculum was too. As Tiffany and Dr. Peterson continued to discuss the curriculum and the culture and climate of the department, I was mentally checked out. Physically, I was present, but mentally, I was in a pensive mood critically reflecting on my secondary ELA experiences as a Black male. My high school English courses were taught by mostly white women with the exception of my AP senior English teacher who was a white male. Building upon the words and similar experiences of Haddix (2016),

> My English courses were taught by teachers who worshipped the literary canon and whose ideas of American literature did not include many of the

English III Curriculum
Literature
(all terms are from State Standards 2002)

Note: Each unit should be introduced with background information to provide an understanding and influence of the literary period.

Literature / Reading Selections in bold are encouraged for in-common testing	Vocabulary	Literary Elements	Communication (Listening, Speaking, Viewing)	Writing / Research State standards require varied assessments. See the Research Topic Ideas folder in the shared folder for other examples.
I. Native American/ Pre-Slavery • "The Sky Tree" • "Coyote Finishes His Work" • "The Middle Passage" II. Puritans • *The Scarlet Letter or* "The Crucible" • "Of Plymouth Plantation" • "The Narrative of Mary Rowlandson" • Upon the Burning of Our House" • "Sinners in the Hands of an Angry God" III. Rationalist • *The Declaration of Independence* • 1 optional piece	Vocabulary words to be taken from context. Sadlier-Oxford books optional.	I. oral tradition, charac. of myth, metaphor, simile; autobiography II. symbolism, universal themes, allusion, the influence of American cultural, philosophical, religious, and ethical perspectives, foreshadowing, figurative language, irony (dramatic, situational, and verbal), setting, mood, characterization, point of view, static/dynamic character, conflict (internal and external), protagonist/antagonist, comic relief; allusions (Biblical); inversion; extended metaphor, aphorism; figures of	• Holt audio cd • Holt fine art transparencies • Holt Video Connections • Graphic organizers (Thinking Maps) • Holt Literary elements transparencies • Oral presentations of original work • Persuasive Speech • Socratic Questioning • Memorization and oral presentation of text Other Audio: *The Crucible* *Of Mice and Men* *Their Eyes Were …* *A Raisin in the Sun* Videos: A&E Biography videos on	• **Quizzes** • **Unit tests** • **Analyze the characteristics of the particular time period using any short story, poem, or non-fiction work studied** • **See attachment for research assignments** I. Expository Writing: Analyze the characteristics of Native American myths II. Expository Writing: • Analyze the idea of piety, hypocrisy, integrity, and fear/suspicion in a Puritan society

FIGURE 4.1   Examples of selected texts and writing activities of a secondary English language arts curriculum

authors who looked like me or who had common histories. Instead, I found ways to relate to and appreciate Hemingway, Chaucer, Steinbeck, Sinclair, and Williams.

(p. 25)

It would be disingenuous of me to say that I didn't have an appreciation for classics such as *The Great Gatsby*, *To Kill a Mockingbird*, *The Crucible*, and Shakespeare. I had a personal affinity for reading and writing. I discovered ways to connect my personal experiences to the larger themes and concepts of the texts. However, I was well aware that the racial and linguistic diversity of authors and characters who look like me was absent and silenced. In addition, critical conversations centered on race and racism were missing from my high school English courses. Although I was new to the game, I understood what type of ELA teacher I wanted to be. Race shapes the classroom experiences of Black children and youth. However, oftentimes, teachers do not address issues of racial violence, race, and racism, which in return sustains the racial inequities that are infiltrated throughout teachers' curricular decisions and pedagogical practices. Race matters—and, I made a conscious effort to foreground race throughout my curricula and instructional practices.

The Absence of Race in the ELA Classroom

During my first few weeks of teaching, I noticed that racial injustices against Black youth permeated their day-to-day life within classrooms and the school's structures, processes, and discourses. I witnessed Black girls and boys getting suspended and expelled for minor infractions. I noticed that many of my colleagues omitted critical conversations about race and racism in their curriculum and pedagogical instruction. It is important for ELA teachers to understand that when we bypass issues of race and racism that we are inflicting racial violence onto the bodies and lives of Black youth. However, we know all-too-well that "racial discussions are sometimes viewed as awkward and taboo or what I refer to as the 'elephant in the room' (the issue people know exists, but do not talk about)" (Johnson, 2016, p. 305). Yet, Black youth are *still* being physically abused and murdered as well as symbolically abused and murdered on a daily basis because of their Blackness.

We should be talkin' about race in ELA classrooms. The school-sanctioned language and literacy curriculum and cannon are not neutral on issues of race, racism, whiteness, privilege, and white supremacist patriarchy. Authors' beliefs and ideologies percolate through the development of the characters, the privileging of standardized English, and the (mis)representation of the histories and experiences of Black people. Literacy, language, and race are intertwined—*race is at the forefront of ELA classroom, even when teachers unintentionally fail to address it.*

Therefore, ELA teachers cannot sweep race under the rug or pretend that race doesn't matter or fail to engage children and youth in critical race dialogue and praxis. When teachers refuse to implement critical race pedagogies and frameworks, the teachers are the ones who are "at risk." By this I mean, failure to teach ELA in our current racial and political climate and discuss issues of race and racism positions teachers "at risk" of perpetuating the spirit murder of our Black children and youth.

This requires the field of language and literacy and English education to examine what paradigms and frameworks are being used in secondary ELA classrooms. Since many paradigms and frameworks used in PreK–12 schools often lag behind those in higher education, many recent theoretical and conceptual frameworks have not permeated school settings. However, this is not a surprise, given that many academic discussions are often largely theoretical and not readily accessible to practitioners. Consequently, critical race pedagogical and racial justice-oriented practices have not been widely applied in school settings and critical race frameworks and pedagogies such as reading/writing workshop remain understudied in secondary ELA classroom settings.

Problematizing Reading and Writing Workshop

Before I entered the classroom, as a first-year ELA teacher, I meditated on what type of English teacher I wanted to be. I knew I did not want to be *that* teacher who lectured to their students for 45 minutes straight about the plot, theme, setting, and/or structure of a text. I did not want to be *that* ELA teacher who privileged the voices and experiences of white writers while silencing the voices, experiences, and brilliance of Black writers. I did not want to be *that* ELA teacher who runs and hides from conversations centered on anti-Black racism, Blackness, and freedom. I entered my classroom with the mindset that something different can be created within ELA spaces. With this idea of "something different being created," I approached my ELA classroom from a non-eurocentric mindset. As stated in the previous chapter, in my secondary graduate program, I learned from a constructivist and sociocultural lens, how to plan thematically and how to deconstruct and construct curriculum. While these ELA pedagogies and frameworks were different from the memorize-and-regurgitate, end-of-the-chapter-questions approaches, they still did not center the knowledge, experiences, language, and literacies of Black people or any other communities of color such as Latinx, Indigenous, or Asian and Pacific Islander.

My secondary English education program promoted a reading and writing workshop model that focused on infusing canonical literature with literacy. We built upon Styslinger's (2017) conception of reading and writing workshop model—she states that *workshop* is a pedagogical praxis and something that we (as ELA teachers) should do. In her book, *Workshopping the Canon*, Styslinger (2017) explains that:

> Workshopping the canon interweaves authentic reading and writing processes into classrooms, increases student comprehension and motivation, reaches diverse learners, and fosters diverse perspectives. Workshop teachers utilize reading and writing workshop structures to prompt students' personal responses, foster the interpretive community, engage in formal analysis, and embark on critical synthesis. Our reading workshop includes time and opportunity for read-alouds, independent reading, shared reading, close reading, readers theater, response engagements, book clubs, Socratic circles, and a variety of mini-lessons (e.g., how-to, reading, literary, craft, vocabulary, and critical). Writing workshops evolve from reading workshops as students write in response to a unit focus, mentor/model texts, or other texts introduced throughout the unit. The writing process is supported through workshop structures such as writing plans, mini-lessons (e.g., how to and craft), independent writing, conferences, and/or writing circles, and publishing opportunities.
>
> *(p. 13)*

On the surface, the reading and writing workshop model provided me the tools to interweave multiple genres and texts throughout my curriculum. The workshop structure allows teachers to create an ELA classroom that is communal and collaborative. It is supposed to provide a,

> classroom environment [that] supports opportunities for students to read, write, talk, and listen in authentic and sustained ways around a wide variety of literature. Students respond personally, interpret collaboratively, analyze formally, and think critically through a variety of workshop structures and strategies.
>
> *(Styslinger, 2017, p. 9)*

However, I immediately noticed that the criticality and the race and gender components were absent in the traditional version of the reading and writing workshop model.

After a few weeks of teaching during my first year, I realized that many Black and Brown youth were not feelin' the eurocentric and white version of the reading and writing workshop model. As such, I had to situate the model within my particular context and center it around the lived experiences of the Black and Brown youth with whom I worked and from whom I learned. Even when we *workshop* the canon, it centers whiteness, privileges white authors, and upholds white supremacy while simultaneously overshadowing the voices of Black writers, perpetuating anti-Black racism, and causing violence to the spirit and humanity of Black youth. This model is still endorsed and utilized in my undergraduate and graduate programs as well as widely used without criticality throughout many high school ELA classrooms. It is scary to think about the large numbers of ELA teachers who embrace this model and think that they have found the *best practices* for teaching the canon without any acknowledgment of how the reading and writing workshop model can protect whiteness as a set of ideologies that benefit white people while dehumanizing Black folks (Matias, 2016). Message. When we endorse the reading and writing workshop model for what it is without analyzing and critiquing the gaps that are present within this pedagogical framework, whiteness continues to be unnamed and unmarked.

Although this model provides teachers with an array of teaching methods and structures, this rendition of it, titled "Workshopping the Canon," in essence, protects the canon of predominantly white authors thereby protecting whiteness and white ways of existing and operating within the world. Taken up in district and state policies, it also leads to policing what can and cannot be read, examined, challenged, and eradicated within the state-mandated ELA curriculum. With this intention, there is an underlying layer that aims to control and surveil Black lives in ways that serve white people. Although, when workshopping the canon, ELA teachers are encouraged to infuse other voices, perspectives, ideas, and multiple texts, those texts are still considered in service of learning about canonical (white) texts as the curricular core. This illustrates the narcissism of whiteness (Matias, 2016) and how white teachers uphold this particular type of narcissism in ELA classrooms. When most texts by authors of color are considered supplemental, the curriculum continues the marginalization of writers who come from racially, ethnically, and linguistically diverse backgrounds and whiteness continues to take center stage. This is a perfect example of how whiteness remains curricularly unnamed, unmarked, and unchecked.

This centering of whiteness in reading/writing workshop also impacts white students, as primary texts showcase their ways of existing, living, being, and knowing as *right* and as the *standard* while the marginalization of Black genius in texts spoonfeeds all students misconceptions about Blackness and who we are as a collective. As a result, white teachers and white students do not wrestle with their own whiteness. Workshopping the canon without critiquing and dismantling the canon builds from the white literary imagination (Morris, 1992). Within the white literary imagination, white literature, literary figures, writing methods, and language are seen as staple, and the fight to eliminate racism remains on the periphery and far in the distance. Refusing to wrestle with whiteness places the onus of intersectional justice on the backs on Black folks but in the words of Richard Wright *"Race is a white problem"* and as Tanner (2019) puts it *"whiteness is a white problem."* Indeed, the field English education and ELA classrooms are grounded in white ideologies and white supremacist patriarchy (Tanner, 2019), which inadvertently sustains racial injustice and protects whiteness—the two things they claim to be against. The structure of the reading and writing workshop model is non-traditional in a sense that it does not push for teaching English language arts through chronologically reading a textbook and rote learning and memorization of authors and time periods. However, the literature and texts used alongside this structure are the problem. Even when teachers implement the reading and writing workshop model from a well-intended place, without the dominance of non-white texts and critical conversations around texts, they are still upholding whiteness and privileging white ways of thinking, being, speaking, and existing. This is not to negate or minimize the work of ELA teachers—in reality, this is about how many ELA classrooms are grounded in white supremacist logic and are intentionally constructed that way by systems that work assiduously to protect white normativity in schools.

Critical Race English Education as Foundational to the Reading/Writing Workshop

What if the reading and writing workshop model decentered whiteness and explored the complex intersections of race, racism, whiteness, language, literacy, and education? What if Black lives mattered in ELA classrooms when we workshop the canon? What if the reading and writing workshop model centered Black youth lived histories and experiences to shape teachers' perceptions, curriculum choices, and pedagogical practices? Utilizing Critical Race English Education as a theoretical, curriculum, and pedagogical overlay to analyze, deconstruct, and construct new curriculum and pedagogy pushed me to ask these overarching questions. In this section, I provide an overview of a sample unit that illustrates some of the teaching methods and strategies of a Critical Race English Education reading and writing workshop. I would like to point out that I understood if I utilized the reading and writing workshop model that centered workshopping canonical literature, I would indeed be *doin' it wrong*. To explain, teachers who center canonical texts in the classroom and who implement the reading and workshop model from an uncritical lens are not *doin' it right*.

In my ELA classroom, I married Critical Race English Education with certain components, structures, and strategies from the reading and writing workshop model. This curricula and pedagogical move created a more robust, dynamic, humanizing, and Black space. To create a humanizing and Black space within my ELA classroom, I began my units with a thematic focus. A thematic focus develops from creating a curriculum that is centered on a particular topic and/or theme that is broad and reflects the real world and the lived realities of students (Milner & Milner, 2008). At the beginning of the school year, my first thematic unit of study was titled *The Makings of You: Exploring the Self in Relation to the World*. After creating a unit theme, I then created a text set around my selected theme. A text set interweaves an array of genres and texts across a thematic unit (i.e., nonfiction articles, poetry, media, pop culture, young adult novels, autobiographies, graphic novels, art, movies, short stories, children's literature, plays, and dance/movement). I incorporated texts such as *TUPAC 1971–1996 Resurrection, Hip Hop Speaks to Children: A Celebration of Poetry with a Beat*, and *The Skin I'm in* just to name a few. We critically read and analyzed song lyrics and music videos such as India Arie's *I'm Not My Hair, The Miseducation of Lauryn Hill*, and Kendrick Lamar's *To Pimp a Butterfly*. We critically read and watched films that focused on exploring the self in relation to the world (i.e., *Black Is … Black Ain't and What's Cooking?*).

Following the creation of a thematic unit focus and a text set, I then constructed essential questions, which were open-ended and critical questions interconnected to the thematic unit focus. Essential questions moved beyond yes and no questions; instead, they were robust questions that

> hold vital importance in our lived lives. They recur throughout our lives as subjects of interior and shared debate. They attempt to make sense of complicated ideas. For most of us, they take some effort to construct and to answer.
>
> *(Milner & Milner, 2008, p. 466)*

When I created essential questions, I began to see how to connect and transfer to other texts with related themes, topics, and ideas. For instance, for the thematic unit, *The Makings of You: Exploring the Self in Relation to the World*, my essential questions included *What is identity?* and *How do your race, gender, class, language, and religion affect how you exist and operate within the world?* After creating essential questions, I created Critical Race English Education objectives that connected to the unit and focused on the goals that I wanted students to accomplish by the end of the unit. Critical Race English Education objectives deliberately interweave English language arts standards with a comprehensive analysis of how anti-Blackness, Blackness, whiteness, race, language, gender, and class function within the content (Matias, 2016) and society writ large.

Richard Wright's (1998) memoir, *Black Boy*, is one of the texts the students and I read during this unit. My Critical Race English Education objectives reflected this particular autobiographical text and the unit theme. For example, if the English language arts content objective is that students will be able to cite strong and thorough textual evidence to support analysis of what the text says explicitly as well as inferences drawn from the text (Common Core State Standards, 2019), then from a critical race English educator's stance, *students will be able to cite strong and thorough textual evidence to support analysis of how Richard Wright challenged inequality based on anti-Black racism, ethnicity, class, gender, religion, and language through his writing.*

Another Critical Race English Education objective I created was: *What role does literature play in the struggle for racial justice?* Similarly, I created writing objectives that reflected and supported the oral and written literacies of Black youth. Because this unit focused on exploring the multiple selves and identities, many of the texts were memoirs and autobiographical, and in return, many of the writing assignments for this unit were critical self-reflexive and autobiographical. For instance, if the English language arts standard is that students will write narratives to develop real or imagined experiences or events using effective technique, well-chosen details, and well-structured event sequences (Common Core State Standards, 2019), then, a writing objective that has been infused with Critical Race English Education states the following: *Students will respond to a critical personal narrative writing prompt that challenges them to reflect on their lived and racialized realities and how these experiences contribute to their conceptualization of their multiple identities and others as racialized beings. And how does my racial background affect how I exist and operate within the world?*

I am in agreement with scholars such as Young et al. (2014) that writing is a form of literacy and is a meaning-making process. Within a reading and writing workshop, the teaching of literacy and writing is harmoniously interwoven and they are not taught in isolation. As was previously stated, the writing experiences of the students should reflect the thematic unit focus and essential questions. I believe writing should also naturally derive from the texts being studied and students' life experiences. However, this belief raises some tension, particularly when the core texts reflect monolithic, eurocentric cultures and ways of knowing. It is noteworthy to mention that the eurocentric conceptions of writing are not dissimilar from the traditional ideological conceptions of literacy. By this I mean, the eurocentric conventions of writing mirror practices of anti-Black racism through teaching writing as a stiff, narrow, and linear process that is shaped by white ways of writing, listening, thinking, and speaking.

In Figure 4.2, the writing suggestions from my former English department are examples of how reading/writing workshop is typically centered around white canonical literature. The writers of this *suggested* writing list encouraged ELA teachers to use *The Crucible* or *Of Mice and Men* to demonstrate how history is

IV. Romantic • "Rip Van Winkle" or 1 other short story from the period • "Thanatopsis" • "The Cross of Snow" and/or "The Tide Rises, the Tide Falls" • "Snow Bound: a Winter Idyll" V. Amer Renaissance • **Self Reliance** • **Walden or Nature** • Resistance to Civil Govt. • **Letter from Birmingham Jail** VI. Dark Romantics • **1 short story by E. Poe** • **"The Raven" or other Poe poem** • "Minister's Black Veil" VII. Amer Poetry • "I Hear America Singing", "Song of Myself" and/or 1 other poem • **Choose 4 selections by E. Dickinson** VIII Realism • **The Narrative of Frederick Douglass** • "Pair of Silk Stockings" • Twain excerpts • "To Build a Fire" and/or "A Mystery of Heroism" • 1 other selection from		speech, allusions, imagery III. persuasion, logical appeal, emotional appeal, rhetorical question, allusion (historical), argument, parallelism, theme IV. satire, conflict, setting, stereotype; tone, image, theme, inversion, allusion; sonnet; rhyme scheme, alliteration; idyll, imagery, mood, allusion V. imagery, aphorism, metaphor; point of view, parable; paradox VI. atmosphere, allegory, symbols; sound effects, internal rhyme, alliteration, onomatopoeia; parable, theme VII. catalog, images, tone, cadence, free verse, parallel structure, repetition, assonance; slant rhyme, irony, figurative language VIII. characterization, conflict; motivation, theme, extended metaphor; regionalism, hyperbole, naturalism; point of view; theme, setting	selected authors *The Crucible* *The Scarlet Letter* *Of Mice and Men* *The Great Gatsby* *A Raisin in the Sun*	• Analyze the progression of scaffold scenes in *The Scarlet Letter.* • Analyze themes, characters, and / or symbols in a selection. III. • Develop a personal creed or *Declaration of Independence.* • After studying persuasive techniques used by Revolutionary writers, **write a persuasive letter or essay.** IV. *See above general essay topic.* V. • Find a current newspaper or magazine article that expresses a Transcendentalist view. Write an essay explaining the connection. • Create a poster that presents quotes from authors and pictures found in magazines, etc. Required oral presentation. VI. Expository Writing: • Identify Dark Romantic concepts in

FIGURE 4.2 Captures the writing curriculum in a secondary English language arts classroom

influential to literature. Additionally, to teach speech as a genre of writing, they recommended that we use examples from Thoreau and speeches from the *founding fathers*—their words not mine—which meant white founding fathers. Writing assignments like these exclude the experiences, stories, brilliance, and beauty of Black people. While texts from Black writers, orators, and intellectuals such as Zora Neale Hurston (*Their Eyes Were Watching God*) and Dr. Martin Luther King Jr. (*I Have a Dream*) are sprinkled throughout the writing curriculum, they are overshadowed by privileging white texts and authors, a form of curriculum violence against Black youth. For this reason, I raise the following question: *How can we affirm Black youth as writers, if we continue to utilize prescribed writing conventions that deny, devalue, and deject the humanity of Black youth?*

Another example comes from the grammar curriculum I received as a high school English language arts teacher (Figure 4.3), also grounded in whiteness.

11th grade Writing Folder Suggestions:

Persuasive Essay: Proposal-
Write a letter to an official, could be school level or government, regarding a rule or law that should be changed. The letter should state the problem, propose a change, acknowledge the counter argument, and refute with facts.

Research Paper/Project –
Using *The Crucible* or *Of Mice and Men* research how history is influential to literature. Use literary criticism and biographical information to show the influence on the literature.

Creative: Speech-
Read literature such as Thoreau, King, or speeches of founding fathers. Discuss elements of persuasion. Write a speech using elements of persuasion about an issue of student choice. Give students time to research facts concerning the topic. Include a Works Cited of researched material with script of speech.

Literary: Response to Literary Criticism-
Have students write an essay in response to teacher-selected literary criticism on a work read in class. Example: Read *Their Eyes Were Watching God*. The teacher will pull five pieces of literary criticism from DISCUS. Students select several and write a five paragraph essay in response to the criticism. Students must use details from the text to support the essay. Another suggestion is to use *Of Mice and Men* with this assignment.

Expository: Reflective Essay-
This essay should be written in response to another submitted essay. Students should reflect on the writing and the process and make suggestions for future change.

Test Essay Response-
Any essay included on a unit test. This does not include short answer responses.

FIGURE 4.3   Example of the grammar instruction and curriculum

The construction of sentences, the mechanics of writing, and the development of accurate word usage mirrored eurocentric and white ways of speaking and writing while simultaneously erasing and silencing Black youths' voice and linguistic dexterity that they carry into classroom spaces (Paris & Alim, 2014). We were required to teach so-called standardized English grammar rules which ignored the linguistic expertise of youth who possessed different racialized, gendered, and linguistic experiences (Figure 4.4). To demonstrate, I created a classroom scenario and conversation between a secondary English language arts teacher and their students, during a grammar lesson on pronoun–antecedent agreement.

A Grammar Lesson Centering Standardized English

Teacher: Today, our mini-lesson will focus on pronoun–antecedent agreement. Remember, you will see this on your end-of-the-semester state-mandated exam, which is 20% of your final grade. We are going to explore pronoun–antecedent agreement through our core text for this unit, *To Kill a Mockingbird*. I want us to focus on Harper Lee's language, grammar, and style as a way to see how she achieved meaning. On page 19, there is a conversation between the teacher, Miss Caroline, and her students. Miss Caroline asked the following question: **"Everybody who brings his lunch put it on top of his desk."** Ok, class … let's talk about why this sentence is correct.

Student A: I'll take a shot at it. I get why this sentence is considered correct … **Everybody** is the antecedent and the pronoun must agree, which is why Miss Caroline said **his** because **his** is the singular pronoun.

English III Curriculum
Grammar Instruction
(all terms are from State Standards 2002)

Note: Focus on creating polished, clean sentences with correct verb and pronoun usage. Avoid run-on sentences and fragments.

Required: The following areas are required to be taught as individual units as well as in conjunction with literature and writing.

Mechanics	Agreement	Structure	Word Usage
• Review of 10th grade skills as needed • Comma uses: non-essential and essential clauses, introductory adverbial clauses, participial phrases • **Review of** phrases and clauses as needed • Restrictive and nonrestrictive • Punctuation – dash, comma, quotations for research	• Subject-verb agreement • **Pronoun-antecedent agreement and pronoun reference** • Verb tenses; **verb tense shift** • **Double negatives**	• Variation of sentence structure • Sentence combining to improve sentence structure • Review of Parts of Speech • **Parallel structure** • **Modifiers: placement and usage**	• Connotation and Denotation: Multiple Meanings • Analogies • Words in Context • Synonyms and Antonyms • **Appropriate use of informal and formal language** • Verb – voice, subjunctive mood, imperative • Pronoun – vague, ambiguous, reference • Misplaced modifiers, Dangling modifier

*Available resources: Daily Oral Language in shared folder, grammar text books in book room, grammar units in literature texts.
* District requirements state that 50% of instruction should be devoted to grammar and writing.

FIGURE 4.4 High school English language arts grammar curriculum

Teacher: Yes, that is correct. In the sentence, **Everybody** is singular which is also the antecedent that refers to the singular pronoun, which in this case is **His**. Miss Caroline could have also said," **Everybody who brings his or her lunch put it on top of his or her desk.**"

Student A: I'm slightly confused. I understand why this sentence is "considered" correct, but when my family and friends are talking, we might say, "Everybody who brings **their** lunch put it on top of **their** desk." I always tell my friends that, "Everybody needs to mind *their* business." What does this mean for me in my language? How does this fit in to what you're telling us?

(Before the teacher can respond, Student B quickly interjects.)

Student B: Yes! I agree. And what about people like me who do not ascribe to gender binary pronouns? I don't go by his or her. My preferred pronouns are they, them, and theirs.

Teacher: *(With a flummoxed look)* Hmmmmnnn … you both have raised some interesting points. Let me get back to you.

(Scene)

This scenario illustrates how whiteness infiltrates the grammar curriculum and instruction, and it demonstrates how grammar can exclude certain students who come from diverse racial, ethnic, gender, and linguistic backgrounds. Further, this dialogue showcases how whiteness not only touches on things that are racialized but also gendered. My goal for providing this scenario is to better illustrate my point that the reading and writing workshop model perpetuates whiteness and how Black youth are impacted by it. This is a major problem because white mainstream English is normalized in school spaces and Black youth are evaluated by it. However, in the above dialogue, the students interrupt, challenge, and critique white mainstream English grammar instruction and usage rules through showing the interconnection between race and gender. Student A shows that within Black Language the traditional pronoun-antecedent agreement rules do not agree in that particular way. In addition, Student B explicates that the traditional pronoun-antecedent rules also exclude gender identities. In short, students carry their racialized and gendered literacies into ELA classrooms and these literacies reflect their everyday experiences and language-identities.

Centering Critical Race English Education as an undergirding framework for my grammar and writing instruction has the potential to create critical writing communities that focus on the social and communal aspects of the writing process, more specifically, writing communities that allow writers to engage in critical conversations with other writers about their particular writing as it pertains to them as racialized and gendered beings (Borsheim-Black & Sarigianides, 2019). I have created a second scenario between a secondary English language arts teacher and their students; however, this scenario illustrates a grammar lesson on pronoun-antecedent agreement but through a Critical Race English Education lens.

A Critical Race English Education Grammar Lesson on Pronoun-Antecedent Agreement

Teacher: Today, we're going to continue our conversation about Black Language, and how language, whiteness, race, gender, and identities intersect. In relation to our unit, *The Makings of You: Exploring the Self in Relation to the World*, we have been unpacking and wrestling with how language plays a pivotal role in our identity construction and connects to our everyday lives. We've also discussed the ways that schools disregard, devalue, and police Black, Brown, and Indigenous tongues. One of our texts for this unit is *The Hate U Give* and we've been utilizing this text to discuss how the writer, Angie Thomas, infuses Black Language throughout the text to achieve meaning. We're going to specifically continue to explore pronoun-antecedent agreement through the text *The Hate U Give*. Before we delve deeper, I would like for you to respond to the following writing prompt:

(Displays the writing activity on the board.)

Get Start Activity

"What Do You Say When..."

Prompt: In *The Hate U Give*, Starr says, "Big D's house is packed wall-to-wall. I've always heard that everybody and their momma comes to his spring break parties" (p. 3). Considering our conversations about language, race, and identity and what we discussed yesterday about pronoun-antecedent agreement in standardized English, what do you say when someone says that the sentence, ***I've always heard that everybody and their momma comes to his spring break parties***, is incorrect because the pronoun and the antecedent do not agree?

(The teacher allows the students a few minutes to think through the question.)

Teacher: Ok, let's take a few minutes to unpack this question. How would you respond?

Student A: I would respond by saying that this sentence isn't incorrect and that it is correct in the language I speak which is Black Language ... Then, I would say that Black Language actually has rules and structure and just can't be spoken any kind of way.

Student B: True ... I agree. It isn't incorrect. I would say that in Black Language **everybody and their mommas** is a figure of speech and in this case, it's meant to be funny. In the book when Starr says **everybody and their mommas come to Big D' parties**, she means that a lot of people attend Big D's parties. This is the signifyin' feature of Black Language.

Teacher: YES! Everyone has raised some great points. **Everybody and their mommas** is an example of signifyin'. Signifyin' is a key feature of Black Language. It's a form of linguistic expression that is grounded in wit, humor, satire, and Black cultural knowledge (Baker-Bell, 2017). So, we have pointed out how this sentence showcases the signifyin' feature of Black Language.

Student C: I would tell the person that **everybody and their mommas** might not agree with the agreement rules in standardized English but in Black Language the pronoun **their** agrees with the antecedent and singular pronoun **everybody**.

Teacher: Correct … this sentence is correct because in Black Language this is regularize agreement. **Everybody** is not singular in this sentence … and, if the sentence read, "*I've always heard that everybody and his or her momma comes to his spring break parties*," the meaning of the sentence would have changed. In standardized English, **everybody** is considered to be a singular pronoun which means the possessive pronoun in the sentence, in this case **their**, must also be singular. In standardized English, the pronoun and antecedent must agree and align in gender; nonetheless, we've focused on how language is racialized and now, I want us to think about how language, race, and gender intersect. I want you to think back to the first day of class, when we reviewed the syllabus and we discussed preferred pronouns. Lately, I've been thinking about how standardized English pushes out and excludes people who do not ascribe to gender binary pronouns. Take a few moments to think about the following question: *How does standardized English or white mainstream English apply when youth and adults are now identifying as non-binary?*
(*Scene.*)

Critical Race English Education helps us to see how whiteness shows up in not only traditional literacy instruction but also in traditional writing and grammar curricula and instruction. In addition, Critical Race English Education pushes English language arts teachers, English educators, and language and literacy scholars to see how gender norms are not inclusive of *all* students. Accordingly, engaging grammar instruction and writing through a Critical Race English Education lens has the potential to create a space for Black writers (youth) to challenge the supremacy of dominant print texts and dominant notions of white mainstream English through the content and formation of their own writing. Oftentimes in ELA classrooms, Black youth are hit with faulty narratives illustrating that the main purposes for learning how to write are for learning grammar rules and learning how to speak and write in white mainstream English, while being taught to devalue and negate Black Language (Baker-Bell, 2018; Young et al., 2014). Given these points, infusing Critical Race English Education through a writing workshop is important because it requires a critical lens and counters the way white-framed writing delimits the voices and experiences of Black youth, and it underscores how language-identity is tethered to the writing process.

Critical Race English Education, Reading/ Writing Workshop, and Family Involvement

As I bring this chapter to a close, I return to the notion of *doin' it wrong*—I am not arguing that Critical Race English Education is the panacea for *doin' it right*. However, just like other critical race frameworks and culturally relevant and sustaining frameworks, Critical Race English Education can serve as a starting point and a foundation for creating an ELA classroom that is humanity-centered and justice-oriented. For example, creating a reading and writing workshop model that is infused with Critical Race English Education allowed me to discover that the parental/family involvement component of the reading and writing workshop model was absent. As a result, I created a parental/family involvement component that centered culturally responsive and critical race approaches aimed to create a healthy, sustainable, and collaborative two-way relationship between families, schools, and ELA classrooms. I will illustrate these relationships in the next chapter grounded in the conviction that we cannot talk about creating classrooms that center the voices, experiences, and language and literacy practices of Black youth, if we do not incorporate their family language and literacy practices, knowledge, and culture into the classroom.

During my first year of teaching, I immediately noticed how the faculty and staff portrayed Black parents and families' Blackness, language, and literacies as weaknesses rather than strengths. During an Open House meeting, a Black female parent stated,

> My experience is based on having attended Timberwood High School (pseudonym) as a student myself and being the parent of a child attending the school. I have found that the school does not treat all children the same and operates with a different set of standards for some kids. I think it is sometimes very elitist in how it treats parents, even at Open House meetings. I do attend orientations and find them helpful, but the Open House is not as much fun. There is not enough time to engage with the teacher and I have observed that some teachers cater to certain parents. To me it seems kind of based on race, sometimes.
>
> *(C.M., personal communication, September 5, 2011)*

This statement captures the voice of a Black parent/guardian whose comments conveyed feelings of frustration with the faculty and staff as well as the culture and climate of a school that devalues her and her child based upon their race and class. There is ample empirical and qualitative data that validate schools as institutions that often devalue the cultural, racial, and linguistic capabilities of Black children and youth, and, in this case Black families. However, I aimed to push back against the negative, pathologizing views about Black families through creating an ELA classroom that incorporated the voices and lived realities of Black and Brown families. I viewed the youth and their parents/guardians, families, and communities as co-producers and co-creators of my curricula decisions and pedagogical practices.

As ways to strengthen our engagements with and care for Black youth, we need to be reflective on our own practices, to reimagine our approaches to teaching, to strengthen our engagements with and care for Black students if, in fact, we are committed to and invested in Blackness and ELA. To create a justice-oriented space within my ELA classroom, not only did I have to incorporate the lived realities of Black youth but also I had to incorporate the voices, racial experiences, language, and literacies of their families and communities. I understood that I could not do this work alone and only within the four walls of my classroom—I knew I needed to be in harmony, community, and solidarity with the youth and their families.

References

Baker-Bell, A. (2018). I can switch my language, but I can't switch my skin: What teachers must understand about linguistic racism. In E. Moore, A. Michael, & M. Penick-Parks (Eds.), *The guide for White women who teach Black boys* (pp. 97–107). Thousand Oaks, CA: Corwin Press.

Baszile, D. T. (2009). Deal with it we must: Education, social justice and the curriculum of hip hop culture. *Equity and Excellence, 42*(1), 6–19.

Borsheim-Black, C., & Sarigianides, S. T. (2019). *Letting go of literary whiteness: Antiracist literature instruction for white students.* New York, NY: Teachers College Press.

Haddix, M. (2016). *Cultivating racial and linguistic diversity in literacy teacher education: Teachers like me.* New York, NY: Routledge.

Johnson, L. L. (2016). Using critical race theory to explore race-based conversations through a critical family book club. *Literacy Research: Theory, Method, and Practice, 65,* 300–315.

Love, B. L. (2019). *We want to do more than survive: Abolitionist teaching and the pursuit of educational freedom.* Boston, MA: Beacon Press.

Matias, C. E. (2016). *Feeling White: Whiteness, emotionality, and education.* Boston, MA: Sense Publishers.

Milner, J. B., & Milner, L. F. M. (2008). *Bridging English.* Upper Saddle River, NJ/Columbus, OH: Pearson Merrill Prentice Hall.

Morrison, T. (1992). *Playing in the dark: whiteness and the literary imagination.* New York: Vintage Books.

Paris, D., & Alim, H. S. (2014). What are we seeking to sustain through culturally sustaining pedagogy? A loving critique forward. *Harvard Educational Review, 84*(1), 85–100.

South Carolina Department of Education. (2019). South Carolina college- and career-ready standards for English language arts. Retrieved from https://ed.sc.gov/scdoe/assets/file/programs-services/59/documents/ELA2015SCCCRStandards.pdf.

Styslinger, M. E. (2017). *Workshopping the canon.* Urbana, IL: The National Council of Teachers of English.

Tanner, S. J. (2019). Whiteness is a White problem: Whiteness in English education. *English Education, 51*(2), 182–199.

Wright, R. (1998). *Black boy.* New York: HarperCollins. (Original work published 1945).

Young, V. A., Barrett, R., Young-Rivera, Y., & Lovejoy, K. (2014). *Other people's English: Code-meshing, code-switching, and African American literacy.* New York: Teacher's College Press.

5

PART I

"We Have to Bring It Real Hard, Who Else Gon' Give It to 'em?": Critical Race English Education and Humanizing Research through a Critical Family Book Club

Meditation #6
Call: *The Black family is revolutionary.*
Response: *I'm not thuggin for me; I'm thuggin for my family.* Tupac

Disclaimer

I've decided to purposefully write this entire chapter as a performance and as a counter method to the eurocentric methods and analysis of writing about research. This chapter is not guided by linear maps such as headings and subheadings. I interweave my past teacher self and voice with my present researcher self and voice as a playwright creating a script. In this chapter, I implement a playwriting structure and format to introduce the critical family book club, explain my reasonings for writing in a playwriting format, and delineate the process of the methodologies and methods I implemented to create the composite characters. In Part I, in the spirit of racial storytelling, I (re)enter the high school English language arts classroom where I worked as a teacher, and I move between my past and present selves and voices. I weave together my 23-year-old teacher self **(Mr. J)** with my present self. To be clear, my literature review and methodology sections are written in a playwriting format and structure. Part II is a continuation of this chapter and also written as a performance. In Part II, I provide a cast list of the characters and present the families and the critical family book club to capture the racial stories of the youth and their families (Figure 5.1).

Thus, my purpose in presenting this performance is to share the realities of families and youth as a way to highlight the importance of creating classroom

DOI: 10.4324/9780429297052-7

FIGURE 5.1   Captures my high school English language arts classroom

spaces that collaborate with and learn from Black families and to provide some evidence of the deep and critical dialogic conversations that can transpire between youth and families from different racial, ethnic, linguistic, and cultural backgrounds. I ask that readers approach this performance with open, receptive ears to the stories of families and youth as a way to enrich their own reality. I have decided to focus on delving into the lives of my students and their families—my research partners as I investigated teaching in new ways—so that their voices can be heard. I believe personal connection is a component that makes this work potentially transformative. For this reason, I ask that readers suspend any judgment and approach this chapter in a non-myopic manner as I refrain from telling these stories in a third-party format, instead inviting readers to be a part of it.

Key Terms

(1) Aside—a single character speaks specifically to themselves and to the audience. No other character(s) can hear the character's speech and this speech is directly for the audience as a way to give them special information about the other characters and/or the plot. **(2) At rise**—the people, props, and characters who are on stage when the curtain rises. **(3) Playwriting**—the development and production of plays. **(4) Monologue**—a long speech that unveils a character's thoughts, feelings, and reactions.

Prelude

During the critical family book club, I noticed the intergenerational differences between parents and their children. The meditation from above is representative of the critical family book club and it demonstrates how parents and youth saw Blackness. I witnessed the different vibes and energy that were at play; and this chapter shows how parents and youth grappled with these different types of vibes and energy centered on Blackness. While we were discussing the same topics, there was some tension between folks from different generations.

On one hand, I was gettin' this 1963 vibe about Blackness, hence the call from above (*The Black family is revolutionary*). Some of the responses from the parents reminded me of elders in my own family and community. On the other hand, I was gettin' this young, Tupac and revolutionary type of energy from the young folks, hence the response from above (*I'm not thuggin for me; I'm thuggin for my family*). The critical family book club is a place where parents and youth discuss and come to Blackness differently, particularly as a result of the different time periods and contexts reflected in these acts. In an effort to enhance the analysis of the parents and youths' experiences, the humanization process of this critical family book club is illustrated in this dramaturgical performance to capture the parents and students' beliefs, thoughts, reactions, and vulnerabilities.

ACT 1

SETTING: In Figure 5.1, there is a table located in front of the classroom under the Smartboard where the teacher showcases children's literature, which spans across the African Diaspora. Children's literature such as *When Africa Was Home*, *I Lost My Tooth in Africa*, and *Anansi Does the Impossible*. At right, adjacent to the teacher's desk, there is a short narrow bulletin board with dingy orange and faded royal blue borders that run horizontally. Scattered around the discolored, beige walls are students' work and artifacts. It is ironic the display table of Black literature is blocking the emergency exit—racism has caused a state of emergency from which an escape is needed (or at least a rescue). Knowledge and information on Black culture and Blackness provide a great wealth of knowledge and empowerment for Mr. J's students. Children's literature on African and African American culture provides a space for students to have a voice and express their experiences. Mr. J's students are able to examine their experiences and reposition their stories against dominant narratives and paradigms. In his classroom, students are not allowed to escape without this essential knowledge. In this classroom, the yearning for equity, freedom, and justice clashes with the misconceptions and stock stories that continue the oppression of Black people. The atmosphere is a contested space—a site that is situated in cultural, racial, and ethnic struggle (Baszile, 2006). This classroom is not only about the historical moment, but it also mirrors the present.

AT RISE: Mr. J, a tall, slender, young, Black male with dark skin is sitting on the edge of his desk. The young man is in his mid-20s and is in his second year of teaching. As always, he is meticulously dressed sporting a white long-sleeve Ralph Lauren Polo button-up along with a bright pink, green, and blue paisley bow tie; also, he is wearing a pair of khaki pants with some light tan Sperry boat shoes. His haircut is short and neat. Mr. J is easygoing but firm, and he is quick to smile. The desk is covered with stacks of reading quizzes, homework, and essays, which are scattered on the top left corner of his desk. Blue and green sticky notes are posted on the sides of his Dell computer screen.

It is early spring sometime between 5:30 and 5:45pm. He is reviewing his illegible notes and thinking aloud about the critical family book club that is about to begin. The motor of the mini-fridge gently hums in the background. The silence and the piercing smell of Mr. J's powdery, sweet, spicy, and strong cologne shroud the room. Through the crack of his door, the teacher hears a woman with a light but high-pitched voice on the phone with her child trying to find the classroom. Hurriedly, Mr. J rises and straightens his clothes. He takes a deep breath. Nervously, he walks to the door to meet his students and their parents. The parents and children enter the room.

[The desks are arranged in a large circle. The families and children are all sitting down and waiting for Mr. J to begin the book club.]

Mr. J: Good evening, I would like to thank all of you for taking the time out of your busy schedules to join me this evening. During this book club, we are going to engage in critical dialogue pertaining to topics that are deemed sensitive or taboo, in particular race, racism, anti-Blackness, Blackness, and power. My goal is for us to engage in these discussions through young adult literature. I want this to be an atmosphere where we all can learn together. (Stopping and thinking.) It is my bias (he waits for a few seconds, pondering his next word choice carefully. Then, he continues). But I believe we live in a racially stratified society; and, to counter these issues, we first have to address them. (As he glances around the room, he notices several of the people nod their heads.) Nonetheless, I am not going to belabor you any longer … with that being said, I would like to provide you with some background context about who I am and how I enter this space.

[The stage goes dark. Mr. J walks to the center of the stage. He begins his monologue.]

I enter this book club not only as a teacher but also as a teacher-researcher, participant-observer, scholar-activist, and as a Black male. Within this book club study, there will be a sharing and understanding of who I am. I understand that if I am asking families and children to share and (re)live their racialized experiences that this requires vulnerability and sometimes pain—and, I must be willing to share my vulnerabilities along with my racial pain and wounds. Deciding not to take a neutral and objective role in the book club allows me to work toward my own self-transformation and humanization through the act of research. Hence, the purpose of this book club is twofold: first, to humanize my research, myself, and the families and children who are a part of this phenomenon; and, second, to counteract the normalcy and ordinariness of conducting and writing research, which is often grounded in euro-American and westernized ways of knowing and existing in the world.

In addition, to a certain extent, my purpose for writing this particular way is related to the findings of the study. Findings illustrate that families and children from different racial and ethnic backgrounds and age groups were engaged in cross-generational racial dialogue, which included critical discussions between parents and/or guardians with youth around topics such as racism, color-evasiveness, police brutality, white supremacy, power, and Blackness as a tool of resistance. These findings also suggest that the critical family book club challenged this notion of safety and safe spaces by serving as a contested space for families and youth to unapologetically name, critique, and challenge white supremacy, racism, and their own biases while simultaneously providing families a contested, yet humanizing space for them to share their racial stories.

In the beginning of the chapter, I prefaced with a disclaimer to indicate how this chapter is written from a creative standpoint that challenges and critiques the ways in which we do and write research. As such, it is important to mention that in order to challenge the conventional ways of conducting and writing research, we are required to unravel how eurocentric onto-epistemologies dominate ethnographic and qualitative research which dehumanizes the researcher and the research partners. I use the term research partners as a way to include the families and students as a part of this research study. Research partners illustrate the bidirectional relationships and partnerships that are fostered through critical dialogic conversations. Smith (2016) explains that research partners help to collect, analyze, and determine how to write about the data.

When qualitative researchers detach themselves from the research, view research as neutral, or adhere to positivistic and uncritical paradigms, researchers are enacting dehumanizing qualitative and ethnographic fieldwork that sustains the oppression and silence of children, youth, women, and men from diverse racial, ethnic, and linguistic backgrounds. In my view, the dehumanization that unfolds in qualitative research comes from the lens, dispositions, and purposes researchers take into the work. For this reason and more, Paris (2010) calls for the implementation of humanizing research—he writes, "humanizing research is a methodological stance which requires that our inquiries involve dialogic consciousness-raising and the building of relationships of care and dignity for both researchers and participants" (p. 140). In this dramaturgical performance, I will attempt to illustrate how my research study worked to humanize rather than continue the colonization and dehumanization of families and youth by providing a space that worked to affirm their racial, gender, and linguistic identities.

Building on this notion of humanizing research, Tuck and Yang (2014) offer a theorization of refusal as a theory and method. Refusal enables researchers to tackle and to counter eurocentric production of knowledge and its formation of whiteness. The authors state that "refusal is not just a 'no,' but a redirection to ideas otherwise unacknowledged or unquestioned" (p. 239). And, for this reason, I am utilizing this conception of refusal to not only push against the dehumanizing ways we conduct research and the ways we present our findings of research but also through the research act itself (Paris, 2010). Although I am utilizing Critical Race English Education and racial storytelling to tackle issues of racial oppression while allowing a space for Black families to share their racial-related experiences, I am also pushing this idea of humanizing through the act of research forward by illuminating this notion of humanizing through the act of writing. It is noteworthy to mention that, for years, Black writers and scholars have utilized a wide variety of literary genres to tell our stories of oppression, resistance, and humanity. Black writers such as Sojourner Truth, Frederick Douglass, Anna Julia Cooper, James Baldwin, and countless more expressed the Black experience, trials, and triumphs through poetry, art, music, plays, essays, memoirs, and a host of other literary forms and texts (Grant et al., 2016).

I'm engaging in the tradition of Black playwriting. Black playwriting is grounded in Blackness and the narratives, racial stories, and counter-stories are rooted in the Black experience. In her book *Girl Time: Literacy, Justice, and the School-to-Prison Pipeline*, Winn (2011) created a humanizing space that engaged incarcerated and formerly incarcerated young girls in playwriting. In the study, Winn uses Black playwriting and the power of performances to tell the stories of young Black girls and as a form to interpret the data. I'm building upon scholars such as Maisha Winn to tell the stories of Black families, interpret the data, and disrupt the ways research writing is written about. I want to point out that I built upon and followed the playwriting structure and format from literary writers such as Lorrain Hansberry and August Wilson. There is a standard and traditional play format and structure; I don't think it is necessarily about the structure or format but more so about what we do with the structure and format. In this case, I engaged in playwriting because I wanted to examine a critical family book club with parent-student dyads that I created as a high school English language arts teacher.

The instructional approach used in this bidirectional relationship is unique since it welcomed parents as learners into a secondary English language arts classroom to build critical and racial consciousness among the teacher, parents, and students. The practical component of how it looks when parents are involved in critical race English education pedagogical and theoretical teaching and race-related discourses is important, and this line of inquiry adds to the extant body of knowledge. Therefore, I examined a newly created family book club, which served as a tool for creating a humanizing space in which parents and students were able to engage in critical responses to micro and macro systems of power and engage in critical literacy practices. There is much I can analyze about the disparaging realities of how family and community involvement is often grounded in culturally unresponsive ideologies and beliefs which view Black and Brown families from a deficit perspective where their racialized, linguistic, and gendered experiences and realities are marginalized and unwelcomed in schools that follow fixed policies and practices that are already in place with little or no input from Black families and other families of Color (see Boutte & Johnson, 2014; Stovall, 2013).

As a result, my purpose in sharing these realities here, however, is to highlight the importance of creating classroom spaces that collaborate with and learn from Black families and to provide some evidence of the deep and critical dialogic conversations that transpired between youth and families from different racial, ethnic, linguistic, and cultural backgrounds. I ask that readers approach this performance with open, receptive ears to the stories of families and children as a way to enrich their own reality. I have decided to focus on delving into the lives of the research partners so that their voices can be heard because personal connection is a component that makes this work transformative.

[Blackout.]

[End of scene.]

ACT 2

A Rationale for Marrying Critical Race English Education and Critical Parental Involvement

As the lights come on, the desks are arranged in a circle—the families and students are already sitting on stage in a tableau. Mr. J narrates how Critical Race English Education and critical parental involvement undergird the critical family literacy book club.

[The light fades on Mr. J, leaving the families and children at center stage sitting in the light.]

Aside: As a relatively recent theoretical framework in teacher education, language and literacy studies, English education, and ELA classrooms, Critical Race English Education's tenets in secondary settings are still fairly new. More needs to be known concerning whether Critical Race English Education can be used as an analytic tool to understand PreK–12 settings, in this particular case, to understand the effect of working with and learning from parents and students through a critical race English education theoretical framework in a secondary school space. Even though parental involvement is one of many debates that remain at the center of various educational reforms, a disheartening reality is many researchers, policymakers, and educators view parents of urban school children through a deficit lens (Johnson, 2015; Boutte & Johnson, 2014). Deficit thinking sustains damaging and counterproductive views about Black students and their parents. Despite the growing body of literature, practices, and policies, parental involvement in urban spaces still remain stagnant. Because parental involvement is frequently viewed from a westernized lens, most schools in urban environments utilize traditional definitions of parental involvement (Howard & Reynolds, 2008; Johnson, 2015).

Howard et al. (2012) argue that the traditional definition of parental/ family involvement fails to acknowledge the cultural, historical, linguistic, and spiritual morals that shape how some parents situate themselves in their child's education. As a result of traditional models of parental involvement, urban parents have often times been vilified because their involvement differs from how whitestream ideology would depict parental/family involvement. Moreover, the traditional parental involvement models intensify the void between families and schools. By this I mean, the traditional assumptions of parental involvement do not honor the voices of families from culturally, racially, and linguistically diverse settings or create a space for them to share their lived experiences. Table 5.1 presents a summary table illustrating assumptions about parent involvement with the traditional framework.

Reflecting on the historical and current conceptions concerning Black families in urban schools and borrowing from W.E.B. Dubois's timeless question, "How does it feel to be a problem?" (Dubois, 1903, p. 2), I now turn to critical parental involvement in regard to the ways Black parents are situated within schools as the "problem." The voices and lived realities of Black families are seldom highlighted in the research, leaving the impression that Black parents from urban environments are *unengaged* and *divorced* from their children's education. Parental involvement is an underlying tenet that should operate in tandem with other efforts to improve urban education. Howard and Reynolds (2008) and Stovall (2013) alluringly assert there must be collaboration between families, community members, and educators. Through creating partnerships, critical parental involvement makes an effort to learn *with* and *from* families and communities. Critical parental involvement family practices (re)create multiple avenues for dialogical interaction between families and educators. Table 5.2 presents a summary table illustrating critical parental involvement practices.

TABLE 5.1 Culturally unresponsive parent involvement models

Culturally Unresponsive Parent Involvement Models

- Rely on ideologies and beliefs that are rooted in whiteness and white mainstream culture.
- Use single modes of learning and knowing (e.g., unidirectional information given to parents from schools).
- Utilize stagnant and mono-cultural definitions of parent involvement in terms of, e.g., communication styles, nurturance, care, and family beliefs about schooling.
- Do not attempt to learn about families in a substantive or authentic way.
- Make minimal attempts to learn about the community and culture of the families.
- Follow fixed policies and practices that are already in place with little or no input from families.
- Adhere to one-size-fits-all model (this particular model does not acknowledge the fact that students bring prior knowledge and experiences to the classroom).
- Home and community visits are usually static and grounded in deficit beliefs and assumptions.

Adapted from Boutte, G. S., and Johnson, G. (2014). Community and family involvement in urban schools. In H. R. Milner & K. Lomotey (Eds.). *Handbook on urban education*, pp. 167–182. New York, NY: Routledge.

TABLE 5.2 Critically responsive parent involvement practices

Critically Responsive Parent Involvement Practices

- Are culturally responsive to families and communities whose culture is often devalued in schools.
- Use two-way relationships (parents take on leadership roles and contribute to curricular decisions).
- Create robust relationships and partnerships with parents and community members.
- Guided by dynamic and fluid definitions of parent involvement.
- Acknowledge, respect, and utilize multiple literacies.
- Make efforts to learn with families and communities through creating partnerships.
- Are based on immersion within the culture and community as an approach to learn through and about families and communities.
- Invite parents to voice their opinions and give their input on school policies.
- Are flexible and elastic.
- View students' culture as a strength rather than a weakness. The curriculum hones in on what the students know.
- Are interactive and grounded in strength-based norms and practices.

Adapted from Boutte, G. S., and Johnson, G. (2014). Community and family involvement in urban schools. In H. R. Milner & K. Lomotey (Eds.). *Handbook on urban education*, pp. 167–182. New York, NY: Routledge.

Research about parental involvement in urban spaces should focus on culturally, racially, and linguistically responsive approaches, programs, and models that will create a healthy, sustainable, and collaborative two-way relationship between families and schools. Thus, there is a need to illustrate what effective parental involvement could look like.

I attempt to dismantle the traditional narratives about parental involvement in urban spaces by incorporating Critical Race English Education in the classroom as a way to build bidirectional relationships between home and school. More specifically, I designed the critical family book club to capture the voices of parents and students regarding their experiences with and challenges to race, anti-Black racism, Blackness, and power. Book clubs have been implemented throughout many school contexts and have served different purposes. Chang (2012) documents that, "as book clubs allow more 'voice and choice' (Daniels, 1994), and provide opportunities for students to participate in meaningful, authentic, and personal conversations about literature, they have become an effective approach to reading and discussing literature in classrooms" (p. 25).

Simultaneously, the book club welcomed the voices and experiences of white parents and students as a way to begin critical dialogue across different racial, ethnic, and age groups. I taught in a multiracial environment; and, I unapologetically created and centered Black ELA curriculum. white children and adults should also learn from critically reading and engaging with Black texts that center the Black experience or the experiences of other racial, ethnic, and linguistic communities. As a result of teaching an amalgamation of racially and linguistically diverse youth, I learned how a *Black space* can be created in a room with white folks. I'm not arguing that in every *Black space* there must be white people; however, because I was teaching high school English I had to create an ELA classroom that centered the Black experience while simultaneously working to decenter whiteness. From being in a *Black space,* white people can learn about anti-Black racism, Blackness, and humanity. Because of anti-Black racism and violence, whiteness constantly eats on the humanity and gnaws on the souls of white folks; thus, white folks can work towards some type of humanization through a curriculum that is rooted in Blackness, *if they are willing to hold the mirror to their soul and speak to the racial ghosts.*

I created the critical family book club to center Critical Race English Education while using it as a guiding framework to read and discuss the novel and as an analytical lens to understand and conceptualize our lived experiences pertaining to race and racism. Following the line of reasoning that parents, teachers, and students should engage in ongoing discussions about Blackness and anti-Black racism instead of ignoring these issues, I created the critical family book club as a mechanism for conversation, dialogue, and praxis. The critical family book club supports the idea that students and parents' learning practices are sociocultural, sociohistorical, and sociopolitical (Haddix & Price-Dennis, 2013). Thus, I draw upon the scholarship of literacy educators who propose that literacy is more than a set of rigid cognitive skills; rather, literacy practices are fluid and ever-evolving, created by our attitudes, values, and social relationships (Boutte, 2015; Hagood, 2002; Kirkland, 2013). Through our reflection of the world and our place in the world, literacy is a transformative practice that can build our critical, racial, and sociopolitical consciousness (King, 1991). I draw from the sociocultural nature of literacy as perspectives for not only understanding literacy as a device that unveils and challenges the structures and systems that oppress Black folks but also as an instrument of liberation and critical transformation (Hammond et al., 2005).

Hence, marrying Critical Race English Education with parental involvement moves beyond Critical Race English Education as an instructional practice or framework in schools; Critical Race English Education is tethered to the anti-Black racism and violence that transpire in Black communities and society-at-large and, simultaneously, it is connected to Blackness, Black language, Black literacies, knowledge, and brilliance in homes and communities. The many accounts of racism that are threaded throughout the US landscape are reflected within various social institutions such as schools and homes (Boutte & Johnson, 2014). Critical Race English Education as an out-of-school process demonstrates how communities and families read societal events as texts that must be critically read, interrogated, and interrupted.

[Blackout.]

[End of scene.]

ACT 3

Room C110

[Because the families and children's stories are represented in the data, Mr. J narrates the background and the context of the critical family book club, his positionality, and his methodological decisions.]

SETTING: The southern US serves as the broader context for this study using a critical case site selection. Michael Patton (2002) described critical cases as those "that can make a point quite dramatically ... that would yield the most information and have the greatest impact on the development of knowledge" (p. 236). The South serves as a key critical case selection for understanding the historical and contemporary dimensions of race and racism in both educational and societal contexts (Morris & Monroe,

2009). Considering the South's deep-rooted historical antecedents, Cutts et al. (2012) contend the South is one of the most contested spaces; and, although the region has shifted, the "power of place" (Kincheloe & Pinar, 1991) continues to shape the experiences of the people who live, work, and are educated there. The study is conducted at Timberwood High School (pseudonym), and it focuses on my freshman English language arts classes. The school enrolled 1,456 students. My classroom demographics enrolled 99 students—45% Black/African American; 35% Latino/a; 15% white; 2% Asian; 2% two or more races.

In the critical family book club, seven of the members are Black, eight are white, and, there are three biracial members. Out of the 18 members, 8 are students and 10 are parents. I utilize convenience sampling (Maxwell, 2013) to select the research partners for this study. The parents who have decided to participate in the critical family book club are the parents of the students whom I am currently teaching at the time. I chose this method because of the proximity and accessibility to the parents and students from my position at the school as well as because of my established rapport and relationship with the families and youth. All of the parents and guardians of my students were given a letter to participate in the critical family book club. I created the critical family book club because I wanted to create a space where classrooms and schools could begin to build critical relationships with families from different racial and ethnic backgrounds.

Additionally, the book club is a mechanism I implemented to put parents, teachers, and youth into conversation with one another through discussing young adult literature in a non-conventional manner, particularly unpacking issues of oppression such as race, anti-Black racism, gender, class, and power. The critical family book club expanded across two semesters—the families, youth, and I met once a month. We read a young adolescent novel, *Mexican Whiteboy*, by Matt de la Peña. In particular,

> I selected the book because this novel helps illustrate how parents' racial identities can have an impact on how they create critical dialogue pertaining to issues of race, racism, poverty, gender, and power. The families and children in this study were from various diverse backgrounds, and the novel incorporates the voices and lived experiences of multiple families from different racial and ethnic backgrounds.
>
> *(Johnson, 2016, p. 307)*

[The light fades on the families and children, leaving Mr. J at center stage standing in the light.]

Aside: As a Critical Race English Educator and teacher, my classroom reflects the autobiographical. That is, I bring my racialized, classed, and gendered selves into my classroom, and they cannot be detached. Instead, they intermingle with the larger cultural histories, struggles, and marginalities that are reflected in my secondary English language arts classroom. As a former student, who is a survivor of a racialized PreK–20 educational experience, I realize I have delicate knowledge of how a eurocentric curriculum negatively impacted my racial, ethnic, and cultural identities. To this extent, I contend the curriculum of traditional schooling reflects the identity and culture of white children while devaluing other various groups of young people

that is, the official school curriculum not only symbolizes racial difference, but more importantly it grounds our very understanding of difference as inferior, whether that difference be raced, gendered, classed, or even generational. This epistemology not only grounds our perceptions of others, but also our perceptions of ourselves as well as our reading of the world.

(Baszile, 2006, p. 12)

Taking courses such as critical race theory (CRT)and learning about decolonizing theories and Afrocentric understandings have all shaped my epistemic orientation of how I now view and understand knowledge. My epistemic orientation of how I see and understand race shapes and informs my curriculum development and instructional practices. As stated in the previous chapters, I extrapolated and applied CRT to the field of language and literacy studies, English education, and ELA classrooms. CRT provided me with the language, tools, and knowledge on how to explore the complicated intersections between race, racism, whiteness, language, and literacy. CRT helps us to see that the racial issues from the past dangle in our present. I contend the way we handle and address race-related issues in today's society will determine how we tackle race and racism in the future. Honing in on race, specifically, the many aspects of racism evident in the parents and children's stories, was a way to confront and challenge dominant notions of liberal ideologies, objectivity, and color-evasiveness while generating intergenerational racial dialogue pertaining to anti-Blackness and Blackness, specifically because those concepts are adhered to and embodied in educational settings and society. In a like manner, the book club served as a space for Black families to be able to connect, to express, and to discuss and analyze how they handle and transcend matters of race, racism, and power. Uniquely, the critical family book club provided a space for white families and children to critically reflect on their past and current racialized experiences while challenging their implications in the oppression of Black and Brown lives.

The critical family book club is guided by three questions:(1) What happens when parents, students, and a researcher/educator/facilitator are engaged in a critical family book club? (2) What dominant, counterstories, and/or racial stories emerge from parents and children as they read a book that focuses on critical race issues? (3) How do parents' racial-related experiences impact how they create critical dialogue with their children pertaining to issues, such as anti-Black racism, whiteness, and Blackness? To explore these questions, I employed racial storytelling as a methodological component that illustrates how our past, present, and future selves are continuously in complicated conversation with one another (Johnson, 2017). Racial storytelling illuminates how our racially related experiences from the past situate themselves in the present moment.

It is important to note that racial storytelling slightly differs from counterstorytelling; however, I do view racial storytelling and counterstorytelling as forms of storytelling that buttress one another and are elements of the storytelling lineage. Counterstorytelling is employed by people of Color as a way to counter and work against the traditional and distorted stories that society holds about people who come from diverse racial, ethnic, and linguistic backgrounds (Boutte & Johhnson, 2014; Solorzano & Yosso, 2002). Furthermore, counterstorytelling is in response to the dominant narrative whereas racial storytelling is not necessarily responding to the dominant narrative—racial storytelling names what is. According to Johnson (2017),

> On the one hand, for people of Color, racial storytelling is merely telling a story involving race and racism without the gaze of the dominant narrative. Simply stated, our experiences and who we are as people of Color are not always in relation to or with white people. That is, racial storytelling does not have to be utilized to counter dominant narratives. The existence and humanization of people of Color should not have to be in opposition to white people. However, this does not mean counterstories cannot transpire from racial storytelling.
>
> *(p. 8)*

Racial storytelling is not solely for people of Color—it can be utilized by white educators, researchers, children, and youth. white people can engage in racial storytelling as a method to wrestle with whiteness and to confront their own racism. In fact, racial storytelling should not be utilized as a method that centers whiteness. Racial storytelling is a critical theoretical method that can illuminate how racism and whiteness are white folks' problems (Wright, 1998; Tanner, 2019) and should not fall on the shoulders of Black people and other communities of Color. white people are implicated in the racial violence and anti-Black racism that have unfolded in the past and present. According to Tanner (2019), when white folks engage in racial storytelling and remembering, they can assist in helping white folks to realize some of the ways they inherently play into whiteness. On the contrary, for Black folks, this act of remembering derives from us bearing witness to our individual and collective past, present, and future.

For this reason, it is all of our jobs to own, recognize, and remember our hauntings and stories. Racial storytelling can serve as a method to describe our hauntings. Engaging in racial storytelling demonstrates how my racial memories and moments from the past operate in the present moment and can linger in the future (Gordon, 1997). Having a critical understanding of our hauntings helps illustrate how deeply embedded racism lies within society writ large and how our hauntings are connected to the historical. Building upon the words of Gordon (1997), "to be haunted is to be tied to historical and social effects" (p. 90). Our hauntings are a reminder of what Hartman (2007) calls the afterlife of slavery. The disdain for Black people is deeply rooted in the troubling past history of Black genocide and the enslavement of Black people. Chattel slavery and the enslavement of Black people still have an impact on the way that anti-Black racism functions in the present moment. The afterlife of slavery extrapolates the multiple ways Black people are still viewed as inhumane (such as questioning our humanity and viewing us as predators) and as subjects that are to be collected as property. As Johnson (2017) states,

> It is the racial storytelling of these hauntings that can lead us to an understanding of ourselves and to feel empowered and free. Further, racial storytelling allows us to confront our racial hauntings and to work against our own miseducation while moving toward liberation and self-actualization.
>
> *(p. 4)*

Baker-Bell (2017) illuminates that writing about our experiences through storytelling is a humanizing act that gives us a space "to reconcile past trauma; bring closure to situations; understand how my past, present, and future selves are always in conversation with one another; and imagine new ways to negotiate, resist, and preserve myself" (p. 4).

In conjunction with utilizing racial storytelling methodology, I created composite characters (Cook, 2013) to help tell the stories of the families and youth. I created these characters based upon our eight book club sessions. It is important to note I created composite characters and not composite narratives; the stories shared are the stories and lived experiences of the families and the children. Creating composite characters challenged me to create coherent and cohesive characters that incorporated themes gleaned from the field notes, data, and other data sources. In an effort to create these characters, I interwove various book club members into composite characters which required me to look closely at the body language, audio recordings, verbal phrasing, and personal backgrounds of the parents and the students.

Although the book club served as the primary data source, other data sources included semi-structured interviews, unstructured interviews, and focus groups. These data sources captured the dialogue, narratives, and verbal interactions of families and youth as well as my observations and reflections upon families' interactions. The process of creating composite characters required me to stay close to the data through using direct quotes or paraphrased comments when possible. I crosschecked the information with the research partners, and I triangulated data from interviews along with other sources. In conjunction with coding the data for themes, each book club member engaged in racial storytelling. They wrote and shared racial and gendered moments and memories that connect to their past and present. This step was essential for creating the composite characters. During my individual interviews with the parents and the youth, I honed in on creating a three-dimensional image of that particular individual by looking at their words, feelings, personalities, and histories. In addition, these characters were developed from my observations, encounters, and experiences (Cook, 2013).

It was imperative to capture the nuances of each research partner before crafting composite characters. When creating the composite characters, it was essential that I capture the distinct voices of each character. I had the goal of creating what Cook (2013) and Bell (1997) call modular stories. Bell (1997) defines modular stories "as stories … composed as a mosaic, a design made up of component parts: What modular design can do is liberate the writer from linear logic, those chains of cause and effect, strings of dominoes always falling forward" (p. 158). Hence, employing composite characters required me to be descriptive and to move away from *telling to showing* (Cook, 2013) which required me to engage in creative literature and writing. I chose three prolific creative writers whom I modeled (Walter Dean Myers, Octavia Butler, and Toni Morrison). I read these authors' work to document and explore the representation of voice from the characters in their novels. I wanted to make sure each composite character had a well-developed, distinct voice that captures the data. Creating composite characters challenged me to create coherent and cohesive characters who could illustrate the themes gleaned from the field notes, data, and other data sources. In an effort to create composite characters, I had to interweave various parents and students into composite characters, which required me to look closely at the body language, verbal phrasing, personal backgrounds, and their racially related experiences.

Through creating composite characters and the (re)telling of the families' and youths' stories, I have to acknowledge that my voice and emotions are fully present. Cook (2013) notes,

> the notion of being fully present recognizes the shared humanity and collective experience shared between race researchers and participants. So in the writing of research, researchers must recognize, rather than distance themselves from, the emotive aspect of the stories on the hearers of participants' experiences (including the researcher).
>
> (p. 18)

During the critical family book club, oftentimes, when I heard the racially related experiences and stories from the Black families and youth, my stories, lived experiences, and realities were present and connected to some of their racially related experiences. With that said, the stories of the composite characters are not fictional narratives. The stories, words, and phrases that will be captured in the following sections are the actual words and stories taken from transcripts, interviews, field notes, and observations. As Sólorzano and Yosso (2002) assert,

> we are not developing imaginary characters that engage in fictional scenarios. Instead, the "composite" characters we develop are grounded in real-life experiences and actual empirical data and are contextualized in social situations that are also grounded in real life, not fiction.
>
> *(p. 36)*

The development of composite characters could enable researchers and educators to view and understand the stories and realities of how Black people acknowledge, understand, and trouble their lived experiences.

Coupled with the creation of composite characters, I employed performative writing to show the lived experiences and realities of the parents and youth. Denzin (2001) explains how performative writing is about the world and how the world is constantly being performed. Performative writing is an alternative research method that enables researchers to disseminate research in a non-traditional way. It creates a portal to allow performers, audiences, and readers an opportunity to engage in the stories being told and retold (Anders et al., 2013; Gabriel & Lester, 2013; Howard, 2013). Performative writing allowed me to push back against the restrictions of how we show and disseminate research and findings. Through the utilization of performative writing,

> Research findings potentially move beyond the transcribed interview text and field note observations to a place where the audience can understand the characters as "acting, interacting, touching and feeling, seeing and hearing, making sense of and representing their lives" through the performance.
>
> *(as cited in Evans, 2013, p. 26)*

I present my data, findings, and analysis through a dramaturgical performance. Based upon my interpretations of the book club members and events, I have created a play in a way that captured the dominant stories, counterstories, and the racially related experiences of the members. The use of performative writing enables me to not only use words but also the nonverbal reactions from the book club members which provides the reader/audience with an opportunity to comprehend, discern, and wrestle with lived realities and experiences that are being communicated (Evans, 2013).

My goal for implementing this genre is an attempt to capture the parents and students in that space, to illustrate their thoughts, beliefs, and reactions, and to present research in a way that challenges the historical ways of presenting and conducting research. I am excited about the possibility of having scholar-activists, researchers, educators, students, parents, and communities engage in this particular study by reading, discussing, and performing the research. Having readers, audience members, and performers read, listen, and/or perform these stories humanizes this particular study and the members within this study. In an effort to enhance the analysis of the partners' experiences with race, racism, and power, I attempted to humanize this study by working *with* and learning *from* families and youth rather than viewing them as objects to be studied. Throughout the play, I use direct quotes from the families and children's speech, and therefore, the play is written in their dialect to maintain the integrity of their language.

[Blackout.]

[End of scene.]

References

Anders, A. D., Khalfani, K. J., & Swain, A. E. (2013). Education is a small part of the lifeI have to live. In R. Gabriel & J. Lester (Eds.), *Performances of Research* (pp. 155–194). New York, NY: Peter Lang.

Baker-Bell, A. (2017). For Loretta: A Black literacy scholar's journey to prioritizing self-preservation and Black womanist/ feminist storytelling. *Journal of Literacy Research, 49*(4), 1–18.

Baszile, D. T. (2006). Rage in the interest of Black self: Curriculum theorizing as Dangerous knowledge. *Journal of Curriculum Theorizing, 22*(1), 89–98.

Bell, M. S. (1997). *Narrative design: A writer's guide to structure.* New York: W.W. Norton.

Boutte, G. S., & Johnson, G. (2014). Community and family involvement in urban schools. In H. R. Milner & K. Lomotey (Eds.), *Handbook on urban education* (pp. 167–182). New York, NY: Routledge.

Boutte, G. S. (2015). *Educating African American students: And how are the children?* New York, NY: Routledge.

Chang, Y. (2012). *Developing book clubs in high school English classrooms.* (Master's thesis). Retrieved from https://tspace.library.utoronto.ca/bitstream/1807/33636/3/Chen_Ying_201211_MA_thesis.pdf

Cook, D. A. (2013). Blurring the boundaries: The mechanics of creating composite characters. In M. Lynn & A. D. Dixson (Eds.), *Handbook of critical race theory in education: CRT and innovations in educational research methodologies* (pp. 287–301). New York, NY: Routledge.

Cutts, Q. M., Love, B. L., & Davis, C. L. (2012). Being uprooted: Autobiographical reflections of learning in the [new] south. *Journal of Curriculum Theorizing, 28*(3), 57–72.

Daniels, H. (1994). *Literature circles: Voice and choice in the student-centered classroom.* Portsmouth, NH: Stenhouse Publishers.

Denzin, N. (2001). The reflexive interview and a performative social science. *Qualitative Research, 1*(1), 23–46.

DuBois, W. E. B. (1903). *The souls of Black folk.* New York: First Vintage Books/Library of America Edition.

Evans, K. (2013). Doing time in ISS: A performance of school discipline. In R. Gabriel & J. Lester (Eds.), *Performances of research* (pp. 123–154). New York: Peter Lang.

Gabriel, R. & Lester, J. N. (Eds.). (2013). *Performances of research: Critical issues in K-12 education.* New York: Peter Lang.

Gordon, A. (1997). *Ghostly matters: Haunting and the sociological imagination.* Minneapolis, MN: University of Minnesota Press.

Grant, C. A., Brown, K. D., & Brown, A. L. (2016). *Black intellectual thought in education: The missing traditions of Anna Julia Cooper, Carter G. Woodson, and Alain LeRoy Locke.* New York: Taylor & Francis.

Haddix, M., & Price-Dennis, D. (2013). Urban fiction and multicultural literature as transformative tools for preparing English teachers for diverse classrooms. *English Education, 45,* 247–283.

Hagood, M. C. (2002). Critical literacy for whom? *Reading Research and Instruction, 41,* 247–266.

Hammond, B., Hoover, M. E. R., & McPhail, P. I. (2005). *Teaching African American learners to read: Perspectives and practices.* Newark, DE: International Reading Association.

Hartman, S. V. (2007). *Lose your mother: A journey along the Atlantic slave route.* New York: Farrar Straus Giroux.

Howard, K. J. (2013). We hear what we know: Racial messages in a southern school. In R. Gabriel & J. Lester (Eds.), *Performances of research* (pp. 195–216). New York: Peter Lang.

Howard, T. C. & Reynolds, R. (2008). Examining parent involvement in reversing the underachievement of African American students in middle-class schools. *Educational Foundations, 22*(1), 79–98.

Howard, T. C., Flennaugh, T. K., Terry, Cl. L. (2012). Black males, social imagery, and the disruption of pathological identities: Implications for research and teaching. *Educational Foundations, 26*(1), 85–102.

Johnson, L. L. (2015). Rethinking parental involvement: A critical review of the literature. *Urban Education and Research Policy, 3*(1), 77–89.

Johnson, L. L. (2016). Using critical race theory to explore race-based conversations through a critical family book club. *Literacy Research: Theory, Method, and Practice, 65,* 300–315.

Johnson, L. L. (2017). The racial hauntings of one Black male professor and the disturbance of the self(ves): Self-actualization and racial storytelling as pedagogical practices. *Journal of Literacy Research, 49*(4), 1–27.

King, J. E. (1991). Dysconscious racism: Ideology, identity, and the miseducation of teachers. *The Journal of Negro Education, 60,* 133–146.

Kincheloe, J. L., & Pinar, W. (1991). *Curriculum as social psychoanalysis: Essays on the significance of place.* Albany, NY: State University of New York Press.

Kirkland, D. (2013). *A search past silence: Literacy, Black males, and the American dream deferred.* New York: Teachers College Press.

Maxwell, J. A. (2013). *Qualitative research design: An interactive approach.* Los Angeles, CA: SAGE.

Morris, J. E., & Monroe, C. R. (2009). Why study the U.S. South? The nexus of race and place In investigating Black student achievement. *Educational Researcher, 38*(1), 21–36.

Paris, D. (2010). 'A friend who understand fully': notes on humanizing research in a multiethnic youth community. *International Journal of Qualitative Studies in Education, 24*(2), 137–149.

Patton, M. Q. (2002). *Qualitative research & evaluation methods* (3rd ed.). Thousand Oaks, CA: SAGE.

Tanner, S. J. (2019). Whiteness is a White problem: Whiteness in English education. *English Education, 51*(2), 182–199.

Tuck, E., & Yang, K. W. (2014). R-words: Refusing research. In D. Paris & M. T. Winn (Eds.), *Humanizing research: Decolonizing qualitative research* (pp. 223–248). Thousand Oaks, CA: SAGE.

Smith, D. (2016). *Finding sanctuary in sisterhood: A middle school literacy group criticality analyzes race, gender, and size* (Doctoral dissertation). Retrieved from http://scholarcommons.sc.edu/cgi/viewcontent.cgi?article=4041&context=etd

Solóranzo, D. G., & Yosso, T. J. (2002). Critical race methodology: Counterstorytelling as an analytical framework for education research. *Qualitative Inquiry, 23*(2), 23–44.

Stovall, D. O. (2013). "Fightin' the Devil 24/7": Context, community, and critical race praxis in education. In M. Lynn & A. D. Dixson (Eds.), *Handbook of critical race theory in education: CRT and innovations in educational research methodologies* (pp. 287–301). New York: Routledge.

Winn, M. T. (2011). *Girl time: Literacy, justice, and the school-to-prison pipeline.* New York: Teachers College Press.

Wright, R. (1998). *Black boy.* HarperCollins. (Original work published 1945).

6

PART II

The Elephant Is *ALWAYS* in the Room

Key Term(s)

The performance in this chapter takes on a somewhat different angle from that in Chapter 5. Here **intermissions** are utilized throughout the play as a way to give readers pause and to make the audience think about and analyze the larger message I am trying to portray. Not only are intermissions utilized to pause for digestion but also for creating an open space for the audience to reflect on and understand the main takeaway(s) of the segment.

Characters

Cynthia Anderson is *a nurse at one of the feeder middle schools in the district. She is a biracial Black female in her mid-forties. She is the mother of* **Jessica Anderson**. *Jessica is a star runner on the track team. She is assertive—not bossy, but has characteristics of a good leader. Jessica is determined and straightforward, characteristics she possesses coming from a strong, positive matriarchal family.*

  Dan Cooper is *a white male in his late forties. Growing up in the South during the time of segregation, Dan had many deficit perceptions and beliefs about Blackness and Black people. He is the father of* **Noah Cooper**. *Noah is on the JV football team and varsity baseball team.*

  Denise Jacobs is *an African-American woman in her mid-thirties. She attended Tuskegee University (a historically Black university), and she is invested in learning and exploring her culture, race, and identity.* **David Jacob** *is her son. His wit and use of satire show what an intelligent young man he is. But his wittiness isn't what makes him unique. Many of David's peers depict him as the "angry" or "hostile" Black male who is mad at the world. In reality, David is not this stereotyped archetype. His friends and classmates do not*

DOI: 10.4324/9780429297052-8

know he is working through the different stages of his racial identity. During the summer of David's seventh grade year, he took an Afrocentric course as part of a summer enrichment program. The course and the program connected him deeply to his heritage as well as his multiple identities while opening his eyes and making clear the various systemic oppressive structures that are deeply entrenched throughout society.

Act 1

Scene 1
"I Feel Like I Don't Belong": Race as an Identity Constructor

(Suddenly, a soft spotlight simultaneously illuminates the seated characters.)

Mr. J: At this time, we will go ahead and get started. *(Looks around with a short grin on his face.)* Each person has created one or two questions for tonight's discussion. I'll begin with my question. *(Pauses.)* Do you share any similarities with Danny, the main character in the novel?

Cynthia: *(Looking at Mr. J.)* From what I have read so far, I feel like Danny has an identity issue … *(Abruptly, Dan interrupts Cynthia.)*

Dan: *(Looking at Cynthia. Dan begins to connect her comment about identity to the main character in the book.)* That's why he went back to stay with his father's family. Because he wanted to get closer to his father's Mexican side of the family. I mean he was apparently well educated. He wanted to hide who he was. If he became more like his father's culture, he would have a way to connect to his dad.

Cynthia: *(Long pause.)* I was thinking that Danny can't fit in on either side of his racial identities—he is battling with understanding who he is as a biracial Mexican and white male. For example, when I go to my dad's side, I am like the outcast. I am not brown skin. *(Speaking softly, expertly, and rapidly.)* When I go to Korea, I still don't fit in. They know that I am half Asian, but they also know that I am something else too. So, it is hard to fit in. *(She looks down, thinking.)* So, I guess he is trying to find out who he is and it takes time if you are biracial. Maybe, it takes time for anybody and any child. *(There is silence after this remark.)*

Denise: *(Surprised.)* You know *(looking at Cynthia)* it is interesting that you said any child, because my first grader is working through her identity as a young Black girl. *(Sitting in a desk next to Denise is her six-year-old daughter. The little girl is holding a Black baby doll. The other book club members turn to look at the little girl. With a timid look, the little girl puts one of her fingers in her mouth and covers her face with her other hand.)* Recently, we moved, and my daughter had to change elementary schools. In my previous district, she had all Black teachers and most of the students looked like her. *(She takes* *a deep breath, worriedly.)* Well, she now attends a school where her teachers are white women and most of the children are white. She came home a few days ago and she says… *(Quickly, Denise clamps her hands together, and she begins to speak in the voice of a six-years-old girl.)* "Mommy! Mommy! *(smiling)* can you get me some cowgirl boots like the white girls' wear? *(Long pause and she looks up, thinking.)* And, can you cut my hair in a bang and make my hair longer like my teacher?" *(The little girl gets out her desk and grabs her mom by the waist. Then, she places her head on her mom's shoulder.)*

Dan: *(Looking at the young girl.)* You are just beautiful the way you are. And, you have nice, long hair. *(Denise looks up and stares at Dan.)*

Denise: She and I had a conversation about this. I went to my bookshelf, and I pulled some children's books on Black beauty and Black hair. Then, we talked about what it means to love yourself and to accept your Blackness in a positive manner.

Mr. J: *(Looking around.)* Many Black children and youth are sitting in classrooms where their race, ethnicity, language, knowledges, and experiences are not being centered and honored. Denise, I like how you utilize children's literature to help you explain the politics of Black hair and Black beauty.

Cynthia: *(Concerned.)* I have a question … do we have to assimilate to the dominant culture? *(Looks around at the members waiting for a response.)* Should we eradicate our culture? Our identity? *(Long pause, still concerned.)* Do we change who we are? *(Echoes of the word "no" fill the room. Then, she continues her story.)* Well, growing up, um, you know, my dad always said if a person had one drop of Black in them, then, you're Black … no matter what. *(With a look of confusion.)* But going to school when there was *(she pauses and doesn't finish her statement)* … they asked me things such as, "What are you?" I would respond, "My dad's Black and my mom is Asian; but I guess I'm Black." Most of the time people would tell me that I'm not Black because I looked more Asian. My father was in the military and he was stationed overseas. Growing up over there was different because I didn't have to think about my racial identities. However, when I came to South Carolina it was difficult for me to fit in. It became difficult for me to identify myself. My eighth grade year, I would racially identify as Black, and people would respond with, "No, you're not Black. You want to be Black, but you're not Black." So, then, I began to question myself because I knew that my mom was Asian, but I wasn't embracing that aspect of my identity. Growing up, I always tend to go with people who are Black than Korean *(perplexed).*

I think 'cause that's what my father is and I really don't click too much with Asians. *(Surprised.)* I don't know why. But, when I go to my father's home to visit his brothers and sisters, I don't feel like I belong there. However, I look more Asian compared to my sister and brother. They get mistaken as light-skinned Black people; so, I feel like they are more accepted. When I go to Korea, I'm not accepted there because I'm not fully Korean. I always feel like I don't belong. So, I'm gonna just be myself and that's all I can do. I try to teach my children just to be themselves. Now, when people ask me how do I identify racially, I tell 'em that I'm a biracial Black and Korean woman. In my home, my children and I embrace and honor both cultures, races, ethnicities, and languages—we don't privilege one over the other. *(Relieved.)* Now, I accept both cultures—instead of believing in this silly notion of a *melting pot. (She makes eye contact with several of the book club members. There is a long pause.)* Who has the right to say who has the best culture? You shouldn't have to get rid of the best of yourself to bring yourself down just to be like somebody else.

David: *(Drily.)* It's like they are always stereotyping us as Black people. When I was younger, my mom would always tell me what to do as a young Black male and the things that I shouldn't do because of my race and gender. *(Looking at his mom.)* My mom would be like … *(he pauses)* anytime we go into the store she's like take your hands out your pockets and stuff like that. Maybe, because I am a Black male, they might think I'm up to something or trying to steal something. She also told me don't wear my black hoodie 'cause they might think you're in a gang.

Jessica: *(With affirmation.)* Yeah, my mama always tells my brother stuff like that.

David: *(Stern with his back rigid.)* Black males are born with targets on our backs. *(Confidently.)* The target of being labeled as thugs and thieves. *(Looking at his mother.)* My mom taught me how the world works.

Jessica: *(Assuredly.)* As you were talkin', I thought about something I just saw on Facebook where they had Richard Sherman's picture, the football player, who is getting all the heat for what I like to call friendly competition *(sarcastically)* where he called out another player. They called him a thug. This picture was split in half. And on the other side of the picture, it was a picture of Justin Bieber, the white pop singer, who was arrested for a DUI, and he resisted arrest. *(Rolling her eyes.)* They labeled him as a confused kid. Even in schools, Black boys are labeled bad and as thugs. These types of negative thoughts follow them. *(There is light whispering between the book club members.)*

Mr. J: We live in a world that views Black children, youth, and adults through a negative lens. The stereotypes you all have named and the examples you have provided position Black people as "miscreants" or as "anti-intellectual." These same stereotypes and prejudicial thinking happen in spaces such as this one *(pointing his index finger down toward the ground)*. It's unfortunate that the educational system does not value the strength nor sees the possibility in Black children and youth.

Cynthia: *(Disappointedly.)* Yeah, I'm a nurse at a middle school here in the district, and I witness how horribly young Black males are treated. They might get expelled … while the other person only gets a slap on the wrist. *(Calmly.)* We left home to go to Trader Joe's *(Trader Joe's is a local grocery store)* and since we were out, we decided to get something to eat. *(She begins to describe her* *son who is an eighth grader.)* Matthew is this tall guy *(she raises her arm high to illustrate her son's height).* A tall Black guy and he's wearing his hoodie; so, I did tell him this *(quick pause).* I don't know if this is right or wrong, but it was in the moment—I told him that he is perceived as a threat. Especially, with the Trayvon Martin case unfolding, he has to be careful. But it's the truth ... he is a threat. Although, in actuality, he isn't a threat, he needs to know how some people might perceive him to be.

Mr. J: *(Looking at Cynthia.)* Thank you for explaining and sharing. You're right— the Black male body is a threat to society within the United States and abroad. *(He pauses.)* But we cannot forget about Black girls and women who are also victims of police brutality and white supremacy. Black girls are also facing physical abuse and spiritual abuse within classrooms and outside of classroom spaces. *(Several of the book club members nod their heads in agreement.)*

David: *(Understanding.)* The summer of my seventh-grade year, my dad put me in this program called Freedom School. *(Mr. J looks up from jotting notes, surprised.)*

Mr. J: *(Rapidly.)* Can you tell everyone what Freedom School is? *(Smiling.)*

David: Freedom School helps you to learn about who you are and the world through books. *(He pauses.)* ... it's like an Afrocentric course. It teaches you about where you are from, how you were treated, how your past ancestors were treated, and how you can work against oppression and racial injustice while seeing the beauty in Blackness. *(His eyes wide with his hands clenched together on the desk.)* We may need an Afrocentric course here. *(Taken aback.)* But, wait, it provides too much truth that too many white people ain't ready for!

Mr. J: *(Inquisitively.)* What do you mean by truth?

David: *(Smiling.)* See that's the stuff they are not ready for. *(Moving his hands.)* They don't think ... or they think everything is equal. If you are poor, that is your fault, or if you don't have a job, that's your fault. If you're ... *(he pauses. There is a look of concernment.)* how do I say this without ... If there was an Afrocentric course here ... it's just too much truth. white people will say, "Oh ... well, why would he say that?" *(Wittingly.)* "Oh, Black people can do the same thing white people can do." If schools operated as Freedom Schools or have Afrocentric courses, it would bring out the white supremacists and racist people that go and teach here.

(The stage goes dark.)
(End of scene.)

Intermission

Through making meaning and connecting with the text, *Mexican Whiteboy* served as a platform in this scene for families and students to share their past and present racialized experiences and stories. Cynthia illustrates how she conceptualized her racialized, gendered, and geographical identities and experiences as a biracial Black woman moving from Korea to South Carolina. Kimberle Crenshaw calls these multiple identity markers intersectionality. Crenshaw (1991) acknowledges that identity markers (e.g., female and Black) do not exist separately, and instead, they inform each other. The notion of intersectional justice is not new—Black women writers and intellectuals such as Patricia Hill Collins, Anna Julia Cooper, Audre Lorde, and Angela Davis argued for the need to discuss the complex intersection of race and gender together. Love (2019) asserts that intersectional justice "is more than counting representation in a room or within a group; it is understanding community power, or its lack, and ensuring inclusivity in social justice movements. It is a way to build alliances in organizing for social change" (p. 3).

Viewing and utilizing literacy through an intersectional justice framework is a pivotal part of the architecture of how intersectional justice allows families and youth to understand their multiple identity markers, how they developed, what they are, and how they connect to our language and literacy practices and experiences. In addition, through sharing their stories and engaging in critical dialogue, I believe the families and children were provided a space to discuss critical issues and become agents of change through working together to understand, critique, challenge, and change systemic oppressive structures. The avoidance of racial discussions is detrimental to all children and youth across all racial, linguistic, and ethnic backgrounds.

Also, in Act 1 Scene 1, Denise discusses issues of anti-Black racism, beauty, and Blackness with her children. For example, she shares a story with the other book club members about her youngest daughter who is a first grader at a predominantly white elementary school. Denise's daughter expressed interest in changing her hair texture and color to mirror the hairstyle and color of her white female teacher and white female peers. Denise illustrated how she countered this misconception about Black hair:

> She and I had a conversation about this. I went to my bookshelf, and I pulled some children's books on Black beauty and Black hair. Then, we talked about what it means to love yourself and to accept your Blackness in a positive manner.

Denise illuminates how she challenges internalized anti-Black racism and internalized standards of beauty with her six-year-old daughter.

Historically and in the current moment, society has viewed Black hair from a deficit and white lens. They see our nappy, kinky, coily, curly, and knotty hair as "messy," "unhygienic," and "a safety issue." Scholars have longed talked about Black girls and women and the politics of hair. In Robin M. Boylorn's piece, *Baby Hair: For Gabby, Blue Ivy, Tiana, and Me* (2017), she explains that, "White folk don't understand Blackgirl hair, the way it grows up and out, or down and long, how it swells with sweat and shrinks in heat—our hair was not meant to be tame" (p. 117). In 2013, seven-year-old, Tiana Parker, was reprimanded and sent home from school for having her hair in locks. The school's policy stated that, "hairstyles such as dreadlocks, afros and other faddish styles are unacceptable" (Persch, 2013). This level of anti-Black violence and racism stems from whitewashed standards about beauty and hair. Tiana's school, Deborah Brown Community School in Tulsa, Oklahoma, inflicted anti-Black racial violence on her through the policing of her body while disregarding the cultural and ethnic connections that play an immense role in Black hair politics.

In a third critical moment in the above scene, David, a Black male youth, calls out the educational system and teachers for their sustained disregard of Black children and youth through the privileging of whiteness and white norms. This aligns with ways Black youth are rarely provided opportunities in schools to challenge and critique the pervasive and systemic social structures that continue to marginalize them; the avoidance of racial discussions in classrooms silencing Black youths' voices and their epistemic orientation of being and knowing. More specifically, this issue exacerbates the marginalization of Black students because white students are not challenged to explore, critique, and evaluate where they situate themselves living in a racially stratified society as well as understanding the roles they play in the perpetuation of racial oppression and white supremacy.

It was clearly evident from the parents and students' critical conversations during Act 1 Scene 4, that the critical family book club became a site of racial vulnerability, tension, deconstruction, and (re)construction. Rogers and Mosley (2006) contend that in order for individuals to understand race, race has to be addressed rather than ignored. Thus, creating a humanizing space for families and youth to name, claim, and analyze race, racism, whiteness, and power opens a window for youth to critically challenge society while learning how to operate within society. During the conversations, concerns pertaining to raising Black boys were a reoccurring topic. To illustrate, in the scene, Cynthia, a biracial Black woman, explains that she discourages her 15-year-old Black male son from wearing his black hoodie out in public. Cynthia is afraid that her son's Black male body will be (mis)read. This can be seen when she shares,

> Matthew is this tall guy *(she raises her arm high to illustrate her son's height).* A tall Black guy and he's wearing his hoodie; so, I did tell him this *(quick pause).* I don't know if this is right or wrong, but it was in the moment—I told him that he is perceived as a threat. Especially, with the Trayvon Martin case unfolding, he has to be careful. But, it's the truth … he is a threat. Although, in actuality, he isn't a threat, he needs to know how some people might perceive him to be.

I want to point out the fact that I don't have any children, so, to a certain extent, I don't know what it feels like to worry about protecting a child from a parental/guardian role. On one hand, I understand when Cynthia acknowledges the fact that her son is not any different to Michael Brown, Tamir Rice, Oscar Grant, and countless other Black males who have lost their lives to police brutality and anti-Black racial violence. She is aware that her son has his own individual identity, but due to the historical and current racialized and gendered experiences of Black people, Cynthia understands that her son shares a collective experience with other Black youth.

On the other hand, Cynthia's decision to make her 15-year-old son, Matthew, change his black hoodie deserves a racial analysis. Cynthia's decision to make Matthew change his black hoodie sends the message that if he appears in a non-threatening way and if he looks "respectable," then, he will be able to maneuver society a little more freely. I am reminded of the argument made by Baker-Bell (2018) pertaining to Black language. She argues that Black people live in a world where our language and language practices are devalued and often pinned against white mainstream English. She contends that classrooms must be spaces that affirm the Black language that Black youth bring to schools instead of perpetuating this pejorative narrative that Black language is "broken English" or "unintelligent," and "unstructured." Baker-Bell exclaims that Black people can change the way we speak, but we can't change our skin. Simply put, speaking white mainstream English will not protect us (Black folks) from anti-Black racism and violence. Applying Baker-Bell's argument to Cynthia's concerns in this scene, we can refrain from wearing our black hoodies, but we can't switch our skin.

In addition, I want to point out that fashion is connected to Blackness. Pritchard (2017) documented how Black youth and adults tell stories about Blackness and connect to Blackness through our fashion styles and clothes. He illuminates how our sense of fashion and style not only reflects and serves as a source of pleasure but also as a tool of resistance. Within Black spaces, fashion is tethered to Black youths' language and literacy experiences and identities. Fashion and style play a big role in youths' lives because fashion serves as a mean of self-expression, self-care, identity development, resistance, and self-love. Building upon the words of Baker-Bell (forthcoming, 2020),

> From hoodies to head scarves, *what* Black people wear and how *we* wear it, matters! Although cultural markers such as, "sagging", "backward and sideways baseball caps", "head scarves", "beaters", and "white tees" are perceived negatively by dominant culture and older generations, this is not necessarily the attitude held among Black youth.
>
> *(p. 60)*

For Black youth, fashion, clothes, and hairstyles are emblems for challenging whiteness, white supremacy, and structures that reject the interlocking and intersectional identities while expressing who they are culturally, racially, linguistically, and ethnically through utilizing their fashion to shape their identity and create community as well as walk freely in spaces that too frequently deny their existence and humanity.

ACT 1

SCENE 2
"We Have to See Color": Color-Evasive Ideology

(Mr. J is taking copious notes in a black and white composition notebook. The members of the book club sit quietly. Patiently waiting. Suddenly, a soft spotlight simultaneously illuminates the seated characters.)

Mr. J: So ... my next question is how do you create conversations about issues involving race with your children? *(The parents and students are looking around at one another waiting for someone to speak.)*

Cynthia: *(Softly)* A lot of times it's based on current events and what's going on. *(Several of the research partners begin to nod their heads and echoes of the word yeah fill the room.)* Um ... I never really wanted to stress race a lot, but it seems like the more they grow up, especially now with Matthew and Jessica being teenagers, we're talking about it more than ever. And depending on ... you know ... what's going on in the news, I don't want them to see color all the time. When they walk into a room, the first thing I don't want them to say is, "I'm the only Black person here." *(She laughs awkwardly.)* I don't think that really was a problem for them until we came to this district *(some of the members chuckle sarcastically)*.

When my son Matthew went to Carolina Springs (pseudonym) all of his friends were white. *(Carolina Springs is an elementary school in a neighboring school district.)* He was friends with some kids at Carolina Springs whose parents were wonderful. I missed those parents, 'cause they were the type of people who would do anything for you. They voted for Obama. Yeah, the mom was actually upset because there's a piece of land that she and her neighbor share. She said it's actually hers, but she lets them use it. To make a long story short, the lady put a McCain sign up, and my friend took it down *(pauses)*—the friends he (Matthew) had, those were the type of parents his friends had. And they ... *(looking around with raising of the voice)* ... they treated him nicely and he went places with them. Those kids came to my house; so, it was mutual *(smiling)*. One day, I was showing someone a picture of him. He was on the soccer team, and it was his team picture. He was the only Black kid in the picture. *(She pauses.)* He was the only Black player on the team. One of my co-workers who saw the pictured asked me, "How does he feel about being the only Black person on the team?" *(Looking around and fidgeting with her fingers.)* And I said, "Honestly, at the time, I don't think he knew or saw it that particular way. I don't think it bothered him. Those were his friends."

Denise: *(Looking at Cynthia, confused.)* You said you don't want your children to always see color, right?

Cynthia: *(Quickly)* Yes, that is right. *(There is an extensive pause. No one moves or speaks for a long, awkward moment. Then, Cynthia breaks the silence.)* Well, I just don't want them to concentrate on it too much. *(Looking around for some type of verbal or body affirmation from the other members.)* I don't want them to ever use it as an excuse … *(she continues to quickly look around the room)* … not to try hard or to think they are not going to get something because they are Black. I want them to always be the best that they can be regardless of their color. And I also want to add that when I was in school years ago, I really didn't experience a lot of racism *(pauses)* that I knew about … *(thinking)* or maybe I was too blind to see it.

David: *(Looking down at the desk.)* We have to see color. *(He begins to look up and he looks at Mr. J.)* Most people who are in power, they don't see color *(sarcastically)* or they do see it, and they don't care to acknowledge it. *(He pauses.)* When most people talk about poverty, they don't touch racism at all! *(Rapidly, he clutches his hands together and he slightly bends over in his desk.)* They think … *(drily)* okay, if you are poor, it's your fault. *(Looking around.)* We have targets on our backs. *(He looks at Cynthia.)* You have one on your back. *(The room becomes silent and the humming from the mini-fridge fills the room.)* white people think … *(in a snarky voice)* Oh why do we have to learn about the Black women and men? They can do whatever they want. This is America we are all equal. Even the drill team at the high school promotes this idea of America as an equal society. Sergeant Major, my drill coach, says we all step off on the left foot because we are a unit. But I believe we don't all start with our left foot. I think this can be compared to America because not everyone steps out on their left foot. Many white people are privileged and oftentimes their feet don't even touch the ground.

Denise: *(Supporting her son while nodding her head.)* We (as people of color and as a society) are all different. We share similarities but at the same time, we are different.

Cynthia: *(Taking deep breaths while pausing in between.)* I am trying to wrap my head around all of this. Because we probably feel like if you talk about these issues—I mean nothing really gets resolved. *(She raises her shoulders.)* Dr. King talked about peace, equity, and solidarity but if you look at the world and our current issues, you will see that things are still the same. *(Softly)* Nothing really changed. *(She looks at Mr. J.)* But I understand you are trying to figure out what we can do. Maybe, you can be the next President and that could change everything. *(Mr. J looks back and smiles.)* But you know *(she pauses)* you are opening their eyes outside of the box. *(Waits.)* Do you know what I am saying?

Mr. J: *(Nodding his head.)* Yes. I know what you're sayin'.

   (Curtain.)

Intermission

Oftentimes, critical dialogue around issues of anti-Black racism and violence does not transpire in social institutions such as schools; in part, because we live in a society where people often view everyone as the same and embrace a color-evasive ideology with regard to race. It is noteworthy to mention that I intentionally use "color-evasive" instead of "color-blind." Color-evasiveness explores and centers the intersections of race, racism, white supremacy, and dis/ability. As Annamma et al. (2017) point out, "Specifically, the racial ideology of denying the significance of race should not be equated with blindness because it is an inadequate descriptor. Color-blindness, as a racial ideology, conflates lack of eyesight with lack of knowing" (p. 154).

In Act 1 Scene 2, the theme of color-evasiveness was a reoccurring theme and conversation. Within school contexts and in outside-of-school contexts, pervasive dialogue, often seen as virtuous, promotes a view of everyone as the *same* despite their racial, ethnic, and linguistic identities. This racial ideology of sameness is ascribed because most white folks are not *comfortable* discussing anti-Black racism and have learned whiteness as rightness, as the norm, thus maintaining white comfort (Ladson-Billings, 2009). Unfortunately, many teachers, researchers, parents, and students internalize this message and sometimes act out these kinds of messages (Boutte et al., 2011).

In Act 1 Scene 2, Cynthia explained that she does not want to stress race to her two Black teenage children and that she does not want them to see only race. It is evident that she has embraced and internalized a color-evasive approach. To illustrate, Cynthia explained,

> I never really wanted to stress race a lot, but it seems like the more they grow up, especially now with Matthew and Jessica being teenagers, we're talking about it more than ever. And depending on … you know … what's going on in the news, I don't want them to see color all the time.

However, if parents and guardians teach their children from a color-evasive view, it is possible for them to internalize this false idea of not seeing race as well as views of whiteness as the "correct" norm with no understandings about the sociopolitical construction of race.

In addition, Cynthia stated that her white neighbors were down for the struggle because they voted for President Obama. Message. We do not live in a post-racial society just because a Black President was elected. From a critical race English educator's perspective, nothing could be further from the truth. And just because white folks voted for President Obama does not make them non-racist: "racialized outcomes do not require racist actors" (Boutte et al., 2011, p. 115). A color-evasive approach and ideology not only blocks the humanity of people of color but also, it blocks white people's humanity in being able to see the beauty and brilliance of Blackness. David, a young Black male in this scene, challenged Cynthia's thinking about not seeing race. During the conversation, David stated that, "We have to see color. Most people who are in power don't see color or they do see it, and they don't care to acknowledge it." This statement from David made clear how color-evasive ideology can be nebulous because it stands in the way of recognizing, critiquing, and challenging anti-Black racism.

In these ways, this scene captures the intergenerational racial dialogue that is demonstrated between the adults and the youth. Intergenerational racial dialogue enables us to reach and look back for knowledge and understanding about race and racism while thinking about the present so that we can move forward toward a fully informed future. We (as a society) are living in complex and perilous times. Thus, it is apparent that generations have to come together to discuss our past, present, and future issues regarding race and racism along with other intersecting oppressions (Baszile, 2006). Intergenerational racial dialogue builds from Matias's (2016) notion of humanizing racial dialogue. On the contrary, many educators, teacher education programs, and school districts are afraid to engage youth and their families in humanizing dialogue about race, racism, anti-Blackness, whiteness, Blackness, and power. Generations have different interpretations of race, racism, class, sexual orientation, religion, etc. As a result, it is clear that generationally, many people navigate and handle whiteness and white supremacy differently, sometimes divided because of our perspectives and interpretations of these constructs.

ACT 1

SCENE 3
"Black Is in and Light Is out": Colorism

(Suddenly and simultaneously a soft spotlight illuminates the seated characters.)

Jessica: In Chapter 3, what are your thoughts about Danny wanting to eradicate his American identity and culture? *(She smiles and waits for someone to respond to her question.)* *(In the book, the main character, Danny, does not fully embrace his identity as an American. He struggles with his Mexican identity and his identity as a white person.)*

Denise: *(Assuredly)* I understand how he wanted to get rid of his identity, and how he wishes he were darker. I remember when I went to high school. *(She scrunches her face and begins to reminisce.)* I guess you would say *(she waits)* dark skin was ugly to a lot of people. You had to be light skinned or even White! *(Her voice gets louder and her eyes become wider.)* When it came to dating a lot of the guys would consider dark-skinned women ugly. *(Disappointedly.)* As the years passed, people started saying, "Black is in and light is out!" *(Simultaneously, she laughs and claps her hands together. Then, she reaches over and slaps hands with another parent who is laughing and making commentary in regards to Denise's comment.)*

Jessica: *(With a strong, excited voice)* This made me think about when I was growing up. I realized I was biracial in elementary school. *(Looking around)* I guess … um, 'cause I was half Black and half Asian, everybody though I was cool.

So, as a fourth grader, I felt like I was on a pedestal, because of my light skin. *(Still looking around.)* If you are light-skinned, sometimes you aren't treated the same as somebody who is dark-skinned. If you are darker, most of the times people perceive dark-skinned people to be a threat, or they automatically get labeled like a thug or something.

Noah: *(Puzzled.)* So, why do you think it is like that? *(Looking at Jessica.)* The Black guys on the football team are always talking about this light-skin and dark-skin battle.

Jessica: *(Staring back at Noah.)* Well, it goes back to slavery.

Noah: *(Surprised.)* Slavery? How does it connect to slavery?

Jessica: *(Confidently)* Roots! During slavery most dark-skinned people had to work in the fields, and most light-skinned people worked in the house. Light-skinned people did not want their kids to marry dark-skinned people. *(Staring at Noah)* it was just that way. I don't know why, but whenever I watch *Roots*, my mom pointed out, she said like back in the day, it was real—if you were light-skinned, you wanted to stay light-skinned or whatever, 'cause like light-skinned people had the better jobs, usually.

David: *(Looking at Jessica and Noah in a concerned manner)* So, how do we see that play out today?

Jessica: *(Waiting to see if Noah is going to say something)* I am on the track team and the guys are always joking around *(smiling)* the light-skinned guys are always saying they are going to take the dark-skinned guys' girlfriends *(laughter from the book club members)* and the dark-skinned guys say the exact same thing about light-skinned guys.

David: *(Looking at Jessica)* How do you think that makes Black people look *(he pauses)* when we separate ourselves … with this division amongst ourselves based upon skin complexion? *(The other book club members look around. David's mom, Denise, is smiling while whispering to Cynthia.)*

Jessica: We are already divided. *(Pauses.)* We're already divided in a way … it's white and Black. *(Dan nods his head.)* And, then, within the Black community, you got dark-skin versus light-skin. I know that we shouldn't disown each other because of our skin complexion, because it puts white people on a pedestal *(long pause of silence)*, which means we aren't really going to get anywhere.

Mr. J: Right, when we create a division amongst ourselves, it reifies white dominance. When people of the same racial background discriminate against one another because of their skin color, it is called colorism. Usually, the lighter skin is treated better than the darker skin. The lighter you are the prettier you are and the closer you are to white. Colorism is detrimental to the human psyche. People can internalize these negative thoughts and ideologies and not fully embrace who they are. If we don't love ourselves how do we expect others to love us? It is important that we learn how to love ourselves without hating others.

(Lights out. Curtain.)

Intermission

In Act 1 Scene 3, the discussion of colorism emerged. Colorism is discrimination or bias based on skin complexion (Hochschild & Weaver, 2007). When people of the same racial background discriminate against one another because of their lightness or darkness of their skin color, it is called colorism. Colorism has its historical roots in racism, classism, and whiteness, and it is an undeniable issue in the Black community. To illustrate, within Black communities, we often find and hear about how lighter-skinned people can encounter special treatment as opposed to darker-skinned people. Lighter-skinned individuals are often seen as pretty, nice, and intelligent (Johnson, 2014). Colorism is detrimental to the human psyche and is anchored in intentionally taught anti-darkness by colonizers of the African continent, the propagandized misnomer of the "Dark Continent" a prime example. Some Black people around the world have internalized these negative teachings and are therefore not able to fully embrace and accept who they/we are. I contend that as long as anti-Black racial subjugation continues to be a problem, colorism will continue to be one also.

In the critical family book club, Jessica posed a question trying to elicit thoughts from other book club members about the main character in the novel and how he wanted to eradicate parts of his identity and culture that made him white. Responding to the question, Denise, a Black female parent, provided her experiences based upon this idea of eradicating one's culture and identity:

> I remember when I went to high school. *(She scrunches her face and begins to reminisce.)* I guess you would say *(she waits)* dark skin was ugly to a lot of people. You had to be light skinned or even white! *(Her voice gets louder and her eyes become wider.)* When it came to dating a lot of the guys would consider dark-skinned women ugly. *(Disappointedly)*

In the above quote, Denise pushed the discussion forward by bringing in the issue of colorism within Black communities. More specifically, Denise made clear how dark skin can sometimes be viewed as "ugliness" and light-skin often indicates beauty (Boutte, 2015; Dumas, 2014). The parents and students then explored and wrestled with how colorism reflects the working of white supremacy because lighter-skinned people are assigned privileges based upon their skin complexion. Take for example, the role of the media and its sustainment of colorism and the promotion of lighter skin to equate to beauty. In popular Hollywood films, advertisements, and within the music industry, the media suggests that darker people do not look good.

We must understand that colorism is an oppressive, dangerous, and violent act that propagates racial marginalization and division between people who are of the same racial groups. The title of this scene, "Black Is in and Light Is out," derives from Denise's racial memory and experiences from her past high school years. It was a statement and phrase among the Black community; however, to say that one shade of Blackness is "in" and the other one is "out" unintentionally and intentionally pins us against each other, and we must begin to (re)imagine Blackness in positive ways that center Black people's humanity and the telling of our stories through showcasing love for all shades of Blackness.

ACT 1

SCENE 4

Blackness as a Tool of Resistance

(The light slowly illuminates the members of the book club.)

Denise: *(Sitting upright and looking around the room.)* I have a question … this question is pertaining to the book*(puzzled)*. How did you feel about Danny's grandmother always serving him first for every meal and putting him on a pedestal as opposed to the other elders in the house?

Dan: *(His glasses are on the tip of his nose. He carries a look of uncertainty.)* I wonder if he wasn't a good student in school or smart, would she had done this? *(He waits and continues to look around.)* I also believe she is ashamed of her Mexican heritage and identity.

Denise: *(Shaking her head in agreement)* She sees his white identity as something to be privileged which is why she decides to always feed him first instead of the other elders in the family.

Dan: *(Turning to Denise)* Danny's grandma believes he is going to have opportunities.

Denise: *(Turning and looking at him.)* Because he would *make it* as a white person than as Mexican?

Dan: I would be curious to know what the rest of the family thinks about the grandma treating him like this?

Denise: *(Disappointedly)* Older generations are hard to change. *(Her head is tilted back and her eyes are cut to the left … looks like a moment of reflection.)* Talking about all of this reminds me of my college years. *(She sighs.)* Um, when I was in college, I played women's basketball, and I had an intense racial experience. *(She pauses and continues to look up. She is searching for her thoughts.)* Ah … um … I think we played Troy State University, which was a predominantly white university. *(She points to herself.)* I went to a historically Black institution, Tuskegee University. We were playing a basketball game against Troy. This was in '88; and it was in Troy, Alabama. They had no Black players on the team; and, of course, we had all Black players. *(Thinking.)* We were winning the game, and the crowd was nasty *(with a disgruntled expression)* oh, they were nasty! *(Leaning forward with her arms folded to her chest.)* Oh, they were calling us all kinds of racial epithets—one in particular, was the word nigger. They screamed that word throughout the game. This was a pivotal event that really made me critically reflect on who I was as a young Black woman. *(She pauses and thinks for a second.)* During that horrific incident, I gained strength; and it made me proud of who I was. *(Simultaneously, with cadence, she begins to move her hands while moving her head to the rhythm of her speech.)* In that moment, I gained a deeper understanding of what it meant to be Black woman and what I stood for.

Cynthia: *(Gently)* Right.

Denise: *(Collecting her thoughts)* As Black people, we don't get what we deserve. *(Still collecting her thoughts.)* The issues from the past still haunt us today. *(She is fidgeting her fingers while trying to conjure up her words)* … we are not … *(softly)* I mean … *(hesitantly)* we are … *(sighs while rapidly releasing her statement)* people always try to belittle us. *(With certainty.)* Now, they do this in a real fancy way; and one way is through the educational system. And I want my children to be aware of this. *(She looks at Mr. J.)* My husband and I educate our children about this. We tell them to go out in the world live happy and free but to remain critically aware of how the world operates. We tell our children to not let anyone steal their joy and take their humanity away.

Dan: You mentioned education in your last statement; can you explain what you meant by your statement?

Denise: Well, I believe the educational system has a way of being very crafty. I like to use the term *crafty*. But I don't know if that's the best one, but. *(Shrugs her shoulders.)* You know … for instance, my niece is a South Carolina Junior Scholar and a candidate for the Duke Scholar program. Also, she is in her high school's performing arts program and is a talented actress. She's a heavy-set girl and she's dark-skinned. I believe her weight, race, and gender impact the reasons why she never gets the lead roles in the school plays. *(Upset.)* That's just an example of the subtle things schools do to hold us back. *(Looking around the room at the other members.)* We know we can do it. Acting and the performing arts are in our blood. We invented a lot of this stuff. *(Pointing to herself and the other Black book club members)* it's you… *(Looks around.)* We're the ones and it goes back to our history. You have to teach the kids; I tell my children to never see themselves beneath other people and to never devalue themselves. *(Affirmative.)* We are all humans. I like to use the term *crafty*. But I don't know if that's the best one, but … *(Shrugs her shoulders).*

Mr. J: *(Surprised.)* What does that mean, crafty? Can you elaborate? *(Staring at Denise.)*

Denise: *(Looking at Mr. J)* Crafty would be *(she pauses)* um … *(in a deep and evil voice)* sneaky … putting on a façade. white people and the educational system make you believe things are supposed to be this way. *(With assurance)* Many times our kids are getting manipulated. They are being taught a lot of the wrong stuff. *(She makes eye contact with each parent.)* That's why parents are extremely essential to their children's lives when it comes to understanding issues of oppression. *(She slowly moves her head around the room making sure to look at each member.)* You are your children's first teacher. In my house, my husband and I are on to this stuff. We have a lot of books written by Black authors, and they are about Black culture, experiences, and identities. *(She pauses while looking around.)* They don't talk about how things were stolen from us. They don't talk about how Black people helped build this country. *(Several of the people agree with verbal cues while others silently nod their heads in agreement.)*

Denise: *(Looking up to the ceiling while slowly lowering her neck, contemplating.)* Um ... *(pauses)* you know what is on my mind? *(Waits.)* Something just crossed my mind. *(With a high inflection in her voice, drily.)* Like how white people say things are better. One evening, when my daughter came from school, she said to me, "Mommy, I learned that Martin Luther King Jr. is the one who made things better." *(She pauses and sits up in her desk while moving her hands. Her eyes widen and there is a high modulation of her voice.)*

Teachers love to teach about Dr. Martin Luther King Jr., but it's from a perspective that misinforms our children. You know what I'm saying? We still live in a world where people buy into this myth of everyone being equal and that the US is fine because we are livin' Dr. King's dream. They are teaching those things to our kids; and, it makes it seem like society has moved on from issues of race and racism. *(Staring at the other parents, assuredly and rapidly.)* We have a lot of work to do. We have to teach our children about *our* history *(she points to her chest)* the real stories ... our stories. My husband and I bring it real hard *(she chuckles as well as other parents and students)*. Yes ... *(she pauses and looks around)* who else gon' give it to 'em?

[The stage goes dark.]

Intermission

Across the nation, the United States has witnessed the physical pain and violence that are inflicted upon Black people and communities. Unfortunately, the racial violence against the bodies and humanity of Black people that happens in out-of-school contexts is in tandem with the anti-Black racism and violence that are palpable within PreK–20 classrooms. In the above scene, Denise calls out the educational system for being *crafty*. This can be seen when she states,

> Crafty would be *(she pauses)* um ... *(in a deep and evil voice)* sneaky ... putting on a façade. white people and the educational system make you believe things are supposed to be this way. *(With assurance)* Many times our kids are getting manipulated. They are being taught a lot of the wrong stuff.

Denise's notion of "crafty" speaks to how anti-Black racism and violence can hit Black youth from different angles, specifically due to hegemonic structures, policies, and practices. For instance, it's an act of violence when 15 states openly enforce and permit corporal punishment which disproportionately impacts children/youth of color and students with disabilities. It's an act of violence when school resource (police) officers and school faculty and staff abuse and mistreat the lives and the humanness in Black children and youth. It's an act of violence when teachers enact a whitewashed curriculum and pedagogy that damage and reject the racial, ethnic, cultural, and linguistic capabilities of Black youth.

Denise's comment showcases how schools can feed Black youth (mis)information that misrepresents their racial, ethnic, cultural, and linguistic backgrounds. To resist the narrow, state-sanctioned curriculum and educational policies, Denise illuminates the steps she and her husband take in order to humanize their children because they acknowledge schools as spaces that dehumanize Black children and youth as opposed to uplifting, transforming, and humanizing Black children and youth. This aligns with the scholarship of Dumas (2014) who illustrates schools as sites of Black suffering, writing that there is "a kind of constant travelling between historical memory and current predicament, that there is a psychic link between the tragedy of antebellum African bondage and post-civil rights (indeed, 'post-racial') black suffering in schools" (p. 3). In most classrooms across the nation, the curriculum is anti-Black, anti-Brown, and anti-Indigenous. However, if families are having critical dialogues with their children about the beauty of their culture and heritage, then this knowledge is a direct threat and can be a tool of resistance to the generations of eurocentric violence passed down in classrooms.

If educators engage families and seek their perspectives, they can use their insights and wisdom to identify anti-Blackness in their classrooms and then(re) create and (re)imagine the curriculum and their pedagogical practices. Lewis Ellison (2017) sheds light on Black mothers' counter-stories—she argues that Black parents' stories are often silenced, devalued, and erased. However, Black parents' voices and stories can counter, disrupt, and transform the context of education. Therefore, I offer two important takeaways in this section: (1) Black parents/ guardians and parents/guardians of color must continue to (re)teach and (re)educate their children about who they are as individuals and as a collective because schools intentionally impede the cultural, racial, ethnic, and linguistic dexterity that Black children and youth bring to classrooms; and (2) schools can serve as sites of humanization if schools, teachers, and families foster bidirectional relationships with families that demonstrate a sense of belonging, critical consciousness, praxis, and solidarity.

Final Intermission

Aside: Not only do my own personal experiences serve witness to this racial reality, but also it was clearly evident in the experiences of some families and children. As with society in general, parents who participated in the critical family book club reflected a range of racial, ethnic, linguistic, and gendered identities. For some parents, guardians, and children, the pain from their racial experiences was visceral like mine. Some chose to recast this pain into praxis, which allowed them to actively fight against and speak back to anti-Black racism. Others chose to explain racial events on individual levels rather than to acknowledge or digest the depth and systematic nature of anti-Black racism. Either way, the book club provided a beginning for much-needed conversations. One caveat of doing this work is sometimes discussions open up lifetimes of pain that have remained beneath the surface for some. It is necessary for researchers, teachers, and teacher educators to be prepared to find ways to support families, communities, and children in working through what can be deemed as a challenging and difficult process.

In conjunction, I believe educators should challenge this notion of "safe" spaces. When issues of inequities and unequal distribution of power are discussed, I believe that atmosphere transitions from "safe" space to more of a contested *space* (Baszile, 2006). My English language arts classroom and the critical family book club served as contested spaces that centered critical dialogue, welcomed generational differences, challenged whiteness, and affirmed Blackness, while focusing on how social and equity issues from the past situate themselves in the present.

At the end of the final book club, we debriefed about how the book club served as one tool that allowed families to share their stories and personal experiences with race, anti-Black racism, whiteness, white supremacy, and Blackness. All parents, guardians, and youth seemed to be appreciative of the discussions rather than regretful that they occurred. The book club provided a much-needed avenue and catharsis for the families and children. Nevertheless, I fully understood that some of the painful wounds opened during the critical family book club sessions might surface again at a later point or be triggered by racist, sexist, and classist encounters. Some families and students from the book club believed teachers should have more classroom discussions about race, anti-Black racism, and Blackness without being afraid to discuss these critical issues and without being fearful to critique various power structures and the many nuances of whiteness.

In contrast, some parents seemed to avoid discussions about race. From my teaching experiences, I have also witnessed teachers sweep race under the rug, speak about race through a post-racial lens, or only discuss the past instances of race and racism during Black History Month. Contrary to these experiences, allowing a space for youth to learn, challenge, critique, and discuss these issues is important. These are critical factors that should be discussed and taught in every classroom by teachers equipped by teacher education programs with the knowledge bases, dispositions, and strategies necessary to lead these discussions. In the hands of teachers who are unprepared, these discussions can easily become dehumanizing, unproductive, and damaging for all students.

Discussion Questions

1. In what ways are our own pedagogical practices and research methodologies dictated by eurocentric research methods and practices? What are the other options that will allow you to implement more humanizing research practices?

2. In this chapter, the author utilizes a dramaturgical format and storytelling method as ways to make sense of the families' racially related experiences and stories. With this in mind, what are other cultural ways that people make sense of and interpret people's lives?

3. What are the ways we think of Black parent involvement? What can we learn from these interactions between Black parents/guardians and their children that can inform how we approach creating bidirectional partnerships with Black families and other families of color?

References

Annamma, S. A., Jackson, D. D., & Morrison, D. (2017). Conceptualizing color-evasiveness: using dis/ability critical race theory to expand a color-blind racial ideology in educationand society. *Race Ethnicity and Education, 20*(2), 147–162.

Baker-Bell, A. (2018). I can switch my language, but I can't switch my skin: What teachers must understand about linguistic racism. In E. Moore, A. Michael, & M. Penick-Parks (Eds.), *The guide for White women who teach Black boys.* (pp. 97–107). Thousand Oaks, CA: Corwin Press.

Baker-Bell, A. (2020). *Linguistic justice: Black language, literacy, identity, and pedagogy.* New York and London: Routledge.

Baszile, D. T. (2006). Rage in the interest of Black self: Curriculum theorizing as dangerous knowledge. *Journal of Curriculum Theorizing, 22*(1), 89–98.

Boutte, G. S., Lopez-Robertson, J., & Costello, E. (2011). Moving beyond colorblindness in early childhood classrooms. *Early Childhood Education Journal, 39*(5), 335–342.

Boutte, G. S. (2015). *Educating African American students: And how are the children?* New York: Routledge.

Boylorn, R. M. (2017). Baby hair: For Gabby, Blue Ivy, Tiana, and me. In B. C. Cooper, S. M. Morris, & R. M. Boylorn (Eds.), *The crunk feminist collection* (pp. 116–118). New York: Feminist Press.

Crenshaw, K. (1991). Mapping the margins: Intersectionality, identity politics, and violence against women of color. *Stanford Law Review, 43*(6), 1241–1299.

Dumas, M. J. (2014). 'Losing an arm': Schooling as a site of black suffering. *Race Ethnicity and Education, 17*(1), 1–29.

Hochschild, J. L., & Weaver, V. (2007). The skin color paradox and the American racial order. *Social Forces, 86*(2), 643–670.

Johnson, L. L. (2014). *Who let the elephant in the room? Analyzing race and racism through a critical family literacy book club.* (Doctoral dissertation). Retrieved from https://core.ac.uk/download/pdf/217675341.pdf

Ladson-Billings, G. (2009). *The dreamkeepers: Successful teachers of African American children.* San Francisco, CA: Jossey-Bass.

Lewis Ellison, T. (2017). The matter of parents' stories: Urban African American mothers' counter-stories about the common core state standards and quality teaching. *Urban Education, 54*(10), 1431–1461.

Lewis Ellison, T., & Wang, H. (2018). Resisting and redirecting: Agentive practices within an African American parent-child dyad during digital storytelling. *Journal of Literacy Research, 50*(1), 52–73.

Love, B. L. (2019). *We want to do more than survive: Abolitionist teaching and the pursuit of educational freedom*. Boston, MA: Beacon Press.

Matias, C. E. (2016). White skin, black friend: A Fanonian application to theorize racial fetish in teacher education. *Educational Philosophy and Theory, 48*, 221–236.

Morrell, E. (2004). *Linking literacy and popular culture: Finding connections for lifelong learning*. Boston, MA: Christopher-Gordon Publishers, Inc.

Persch, J. A. (2013, September 10). School that barred 7-year-old's dreadlocks changes dress-code policy. Retrieved from https://www.today.com/parents/school-barred-7-year-olds-dreadlocks-changes-dress-code-policy-8C11122821

Pritchard, E. D. (2017). *Fashioning lives: Black queers and the politics of literacy*. Carbondale, IL: Southern Illinois University Press.

Rogers, R., & Mosley, M. (2006). Racial literacy in a second-grade classroom: Critical race theory, whiteness studies, and literacy research. *Reading Research Quarterly, 41*, 462–495.

LOVE LETTER III

Promised Land

Promised Land,

You are an ancestor, elder, teacher, parent, guardian, provider, and a nurturer who is continuously molding and (re)defining who I am. You helped me to discover the multiple parts of myself. I learned about the dark parts of myself that had to fight at times to protect my Black male body, which wasn't protected in the world that existed outside of you. I discovered the light parts of me where I learned how to breathe love from my heart and express love as an action-oriented process. You are more than my hood. The more I connect with my selves—the more I connect with you. Thank you for being a Black space that sheds an abundance of love on Blackness, creates a space of resistance, and promotes the celebration of Black culture.

I love everything about you—from the tall pine trees to the sturdy oak trees— to the sun-kissed black roads—from the smell of the morning dew to the piercing sound of crickets in the wind—and to the soft and loud ebb of cars moving by. Through you, I first witnessed the dynamism and fluidity of Blackness. And I captured the multiple variations of Blackness in a 30-minute walk. I witnessed this dynamism and fluidity through the hustle of the neighborhood Candy Lady whose kitchen was stocked with popsicles, WarHeads, juice, chips, sodas, nachos, and Little Debbie Cakes. In return, I saw the hustle and grind that resided within Black children and how we would make monetary deals with adults, as a way to get a dollar or two so that we could visit the Candy Lady. I saw the dynamism through other Black children who had large imaginations and who were thinking of Black futures. I witnessed this dynamism and fluidity through the Black women who would be choppin' it up with one another on the front porch. I saw this fluidity through the neighborhood cookouts and card parties. You showed me a Black world.

DOI: 10.4324/9780429297052-9

I have always been fascinated by you because when I'm with you there is no erasure of Blackness or Black beauty. Immediately, I recognized that it was a different story of Blackness being told and represented than what I saw at school. It was a different story of Blackness being told and represented than what I witnessed from growing up in a small, racially segregated town. But I'm not here to speak about the anti-Black racism and violence that occur in my hometown of Edgefield, South Carolina. I'm not here to speak about how the only high school in the district did not have its first integrated prom until 2002. Nor am I here to speak about the klansmen gathering in town square to hand out flyers with an image of a burning cross. I'm not here to speak about how the high school I attended is named after a white nationalist and segregationist. Nor am I here to speak about the high school's nickname which is the Strom Thurmond "rebels" which symbolizes the confederate south and the dehumanization of Black people. I want to speak about the resistance, determination, and knowledge I acquired from you. I want to speak about the power and beauty that live in your name. Promised Land, you are a place of happiness, solitude, serenity, joy, and love. You are a place where dreams come true—a place that taught me how to freedom dream.

Promised Land, you are my Mecca. My Zion. My ancestors dreamed and imagined something different. They were imagining Black futures and fighting for a better tomorrow, a promised land, a Zion, a Mecca. A place that started as a plantation was purchased by the people whose blood, sweat, pain, tears, determination, love, resistance, and joy are deeply rooted in the dark soil that makes up your body. The determination, love, resistance, and joy that I have is because of you and my ancestors who dreamed, loved, and imagined. Now, it is my time to freedom dream, imagine, love, and create for our future children.

Love,
LLJ

7

B(L)ACK TO THE FUTURE

Black Rage, Radical Love, and the Radical Imagination

Meditation #7

When you imagine a perfect world, what does that perfect world look like? How does it smell? How does it feel? (*Using an artistic medium, sketch your perfect world. Utilize words and/or phrases to enhance your illustration.*)

Black Rage

Returning to the notion of Black rage, my Black rage stems from living in a world that dehumanizes and devalues Black lives. A good portion of my Black rage is in response to the US public education system which is built upon white supremacy, toxicity, and anti-Black racism. As hooks (1995) reminds us, "it is important that everyone in the United States understands that white supremacy promotes, encourages, and condones all manner of violence against Black people" (p. 22). In the same way, "my Black rage has propelled me to think about my teaching and pedagogical practices as things that resist and subvert the traditional curricula and pedagogies" (Johnson, 2017, p. 6). My curricular choices and pedagogical moves are fueled by Black rage; and, in turn, I aim to create classrooms spaces where self-transformation, Blackness, humanity, and liberation are centered. Critical Race English Education is partially in response to the white rage that infiltrates educational spaces and ELA classrooms.

I believe I'm on the same wavelength as Love (2019), who argues that we cannot have conversations about white supremacy and how it functions without discussing and explicating white rage. Throughout this book, I've illustrated various examples of how white rage, white supremacy, and anti-Black racism live and breathe within the heart of the US educational system and throughout society. Historically and in our current political context, we have witnessed Black youth and adults take action

DOI: 10.4324/9780429297052-10

against white supremacy, white rage, and anti-Blackness. On June 27, 2015, Bree Newsome climbed a flagpole at the South Carolina Statehouse in Columbia, SC, to remove the confederate battle flag. As someone who has lived in Columbia, SC, there were numerous fights for the removal of the confederate flag. As Newsome reminds us, the waving of that flag was a constant reminder and an "ominous symbol" of racism (Aloi, 2019). Bree Newsome put her Black female body and life on the frontline, after Dylan Roof murdered nine Black people at the African Methodist Episcopal Church (also known as Mother Emanuel): Rev. Clementa C. Pinckney, Cynthia Marie Graham Hurd, Susie Jackson, Ethel Lee Lance, DePayne Middleton-Doctor, Tywanza Sanders, Daniel L. Simmons, Rev. Sharonda Coleman-Singleton, and Myra Thompson. During the annual Martin Luther King Jr. Commemorative Lecture at Cornell University, Bree Newsome contended that after the death of the nine Black parishioners, "there was a renewed sense of outrage over the state's continued endorsement of this hate symbol" (Aloi, 2019, p. 1).

Black rage is activism. Throughout the various historical and current day justice-oriented movements, Black youth and other youth of color have been at the forefront of the revolution, challenging and dismantling whiteness, white supremacy, and white rage in educational settings. In May 2019, at Wilson High School in Southwest Portland, OR, the Black Student Union staged a student-led walkout and protest in response to the nonchalant and lackluster responses to anti-Black racism, racial violence, and racial incidents that unfolded on their campus (Campuzano, 2019). In April 2019, a white student at Wilson High School screamed the word nigger at a group of Black males. A video of the racial incident began spreading on social media. This was the last straw for the Black youth at Wilson High School exacerbated by the fact that, even though Black students were targeted through white rage, whiteness, and white supremacy, the school's administration, faculty, and staff still found ways to protect their white students, white rage, and whiteness. Aslan Newson, a Black and American Indian student, led the Black Student Union. During an interview, Aslan exclaimed, "students of color at Wilson are fed up. I'm done prioritizing white comfort when we should be prioritizing the safety of people of color" (Campuzano, 2019, p. 1). The racially related incidents discussed above are not in isolation from the many other racially related incidents that have unfolded in other PreK–20 settings, nationally and internationally.

Radical Love

Returning to the connection of Critical Race English Education and Black rage, Critical Race English Education sheds light on the racial violence and anti-Black racism that happen in school spaces and outside-of-school spaces. However, even in the midst of racial chaos and turmoil, Black children, youth, and adults have to continue to engage in self-love and continue to love on Blackness. The above examples of Black rage illuminate a radical love for Blackness and for Black lives. Although Critical Race English Education explicates the intersections of race, anti-Black racism, violence, language, literacy, and Blackness, simultaneously, it sheds love and light on Blackness. Not only does Black rage undergird Critical Race English Education but also radical love. Throughout ELA classrooms, Black youth are saturated with fragmented information about Blackness, Black Language, and Black literacies. As such, Critical Race English Education signifies what it means to deliberately love on Blackness and Black people. Critical Race English Education is a call for radical love in ELA classrooms, language and literacy studies, and English education. This radical love for Blackness and for Black life must run through the heart of teachers' curricular decisions and pedagogical practices. A radical love is not soft. A radical love is not mushy. A radical love is hard and is political resistance against violence and white supremacy. Furthermore, radical love "works against the self-hate and miseducation that often begins in schools" (Johnson et al., 2019, p. 56). Aiming to create an ethic of radical love, Critical Race English Education is a racial justice and anti-racist framework that shakes the foundation of the state-sanctioned curriculum, methods, and research. Lyiscott (2019) writes, "what's love got to do with it? Love is the revolutionary act that we are placing our hope in. What's love got to do with it? Love is our call to reimagine a system that is broken" (p. 4). In similar vein, Callier and Hill (2019) ask, "how do we demonstrate our love of Blackness in our teaching and research?" (p. 96). This love for Blackness that is deeply rooted in radical love is a pedagogical practice and action that should be expressed in the field of education writ large.

Black youth must be given the space to showcase their joy, hurt, pain, frustration, love, freedom, heritage, history, and brilliance. There are ELA educators who work against and dismantle the traditional ways of teaching ELA. Shipp (2017), for example, argues that if ELA classrooms revolutionize the traditional literary canon, then, essentially, we are revolutionizing the English classroom. Therefore, "let us shift from focusing exclusively on required texts to equally acknowledging the urgent need for consciousness and activism from our students" (Shipp, 2017, p. 39). Shipp engages in an autobiographical narrative of her experiences teaching high school English in the wake of racial violence and injustices. The author demonstrates how she infuses Black music and Black artists (e.g., Kendrick Lamar and Beyoncé) into her curriculum, not only as a means for teaching ELA skills such as literary devices, figurative language, and literary analysis, but also to engage youth in critical discussions pertaining to the United States' past and current-day issues with racial inequities. In addition, Shipp also incorporates present-day cultural movements like #BlackLivesMatter, Black Is Beautiful, #BlackGirlMagic, and #BlackExcellence into her English classroom, as well as Black contemporary authors, artists, poets, orators, and activists invoking powerful symbols and messages pertaining to Blackness, literacy, language, culture, and humanity.

In another example of radical Black love as literacy, Muhammad et al. (2017) examined the textual, communal, and sociopolitical partnerships of kinship writing as

Black youth composed protest poetry, identifying ways that the students' writing carried "significance in the Black literary community as the history of Black education has been interlaced with ideals of social learning, community, family, and kinship" (p. 347). Through a four-week summer writing program, the authors engaged 15 Black youth in sociopolitical writing workshops that centered on anti-Blackness, Blackness, Black love, and solidarity. Their research demonstrates what it looks like to create critical writing pedagogies for youth by incorporating texts from the Black protest movements and from the past to our current historical insurgence known as the #BlackLivesMatter movement. By critically reading and engaging with Black youths' kinship poems, the authors found that the Black youth wrote across various topics that affect Black people and communities (e.g., gun violence and police brutality, the distorted depictions of Black lives, the conceptions of Black beauty, and the importance of revolutionary love and freedom). The authors call for English education classrooms to move from a narrow, linear approach to one that educates Black youth on how to use their words and "pens" as epistemic weapons to speak back to and against racial oppression and marginalization. When Black lives are continuously surveilled and under attack, this is the time for radical teaching and learning. Thus, embodying and practicing radical love in classrooms is wedded to the radical imagination and the (re) imagining of the world that we all long to see but that is not yet.

The Radical Imagination

In light of the radical imagination, Stovall (2017) argues that living within the radical imaginary "seeks to understand the world in its current state while vehemently working with others to change the current condition" (p. 52). Embodying the radical imagination assists us in understanding how the past issues of anti-Black racism, linguistic violence, white supremacist patriarchy, classism, homophobia, and xenophobia rest in the current moment while intentionally working to radically transform our current contexts in order to create a more justice-oriented and equitable present and future. In scholar-activist Robin D. G. Kelley's profound text, *Freedom Dreams: The Black Radical Imagination* (2002), he argues that imagining those futures is essential because,

> without new visions, we don't know what to build, only what to knock down. We not only end up confused, rudderless, and cynical, but we forget that making a revolution is not a series of clever maneuvers and tactics but a process that can and must transform us.

(p. xii)

Similarly, Love (2019) explains how our ancestors and elders are/were filled with Black joy, radical love, and resistance, but also imagination for what can be. She writes:

> We need imagination. Arguably, abolitionists' greatest tools against injustice were their imaginations. Their imaginations fueled their resistance.

Imagining being free, imagining reading, imagining marrying the love of your life, imagining your children being free, imagining life and not death, imagining seeing the world, and imagining freedom.

(p. 102)

In harmony with Love (2019) and Kelley (2002), ELA classrooms need imagination. Specifically, ELA classrooms must create spaces that consider Black youths' futures. We cannot envision or (re)imagine a future, without acknowledging, honoring, humanizing, and centering Blackness and Black lives. Black youth deserve ELA classrooms that are rooted in Black literacies and that reflect the spirit, lives, knowledge, and humanity in Blackness. Black youths' Black literacies should not be minimized or ridiculed. In the spirit of the radical imagination, educators need to recognize how Black youths' Black literacies are glimpses into the future. Further, when Black youth are allowed to express their Black literacies, the classroom becomes a space where they do more than survive, and it becomes a space where Black youth can thrive (Love, 2019). Black youths' future self is ever-evolving and ever-changing; they need to believe and witness that classrooms can be spaces where their past, present, and future selves will be fully celebrated, loved, and humanized.

Critical Race English Education: New Visions, New Possibilities is about the struggle, violence, and anti-Black racism that permeate ELA classrooms and society at large. This book is about new visions and new possibilities for Black youth. Even though Black youth are maneuvering a racially stratified society that doesn't see them as human, they still possess and practice joy—Black joy. In her 2019 live album titled *Homecoming*, Beyoncé reminds the people that Black joy is filled with "so much damn swag." She asserts,

and the amount of swag is just limitless, like ... the things that these young people can do with their bodies and the music they can play and the drumrolls and the haircuts and the bodies and the ... it's just not right. It's just so much damn swag.

(Knowles-Carter, 2019, track number 6)

We see Black graduates swag surfing during high school and college graduations as the epitome and embodiment of Black joy. When I say Black joy, I'm referring to the type of joy that "originates in resistance, joy that is discovered in making a way out of no way, joy that is uncovered when you know how to love yourself and others" (Love, 2019, p. 15). Black joy is when Black folks actively work to stay human through showcasing an unapologetic love for Blackness, Black beauty, and Black life. Black joy is the prototype for creating a better tomorrow—we can't demand the world we want to see without Black joy, and we can't embrace Black joy without embodying the radical imagination.

Closing Meditation

Revisit your sketch from the interactive meditation that was provided at the beginning of the chapter and meditate on the following question: How do joy, radical love, and Black futures fit into your perfect world?

References

Aloi, D. (2019, December 13). Bree Newsome: 'Everyone has a role to play'. *Cornell Chronicle*. Retrieved from https://news.cornell.edu/stories/2019/02/bree-newsome-everyone-has-role-play.

Callier, D. M., & Hill, D. C. (2019). *Who look at Me?!: Shifting the gaze of education through Blackness, queerness, and the body*. Danvers, MA: Brill and Sense.

Campuzano, E. (2019, May 28). Portland high school students walk out, say they're fed up with lackluster responses to racist incidents. *The Oregonian/OregonLive*. Retrieved from https://www.oregonlive.com/education/2019/05/portland-high-school-students-walk-out-say-theyre-fed-up-with-lackluster-responses-to-racist-incident.html.

hooks, b. (1995). *Killing rage: Ending racism*. New York: Henry Holt and Company Inc.

Johnson, L. L. (2017). The racial hauntings of one Black male professor and the disturbance of the self(ves): Self-actualization and racial storytelling as pedagogical practices. *Journal of Literacy Research, 49*(4), 1–27.

Johnson, L. L., Bryan, N., & Boutte, G. (2019). Show Us the Love: Revolutionary Teaching in (Un)Critical Times. *The Urban Review, 51*(1), 46–64. doi:10.1007/s11256-018-0488-3

Kelley, R. D. G. (2002). *Freedom dreams: The Black radical imagination*. Boston, MA: Beacon Press.

Knowles-Carter, B. (2019). So much damn swag interlude. In *Homecoming: The live album*. Los Angeles, CA: Parkwood; Columbia Records.

Love, B. L. (2019). *We want to do more than survive: Abolitionist teaching and the pursuit of educational freedom*. Boston, MA: Beacon Press.

Lyiscott, J. (2019). The quest to be love(d) in urban schools: Issue introduction. *The Urban Review, 51*, 1–4.

Muhammad, G. E., Chisholm, M. G., & Starks, F. D. (2017). Exploring #BlackLivesMatter and sociopolitical relationships through kinship writing. *English Teaching: Practice & Critique, 16*(3), 347–362.

Shipp, L. (2017). Revolutionizing the English classroom through consciousness, justice, and self-awareness. *English Journal, 106*(4), 35–40.

Stovall, D. (2017). Freedom as aspirational and fugitive: A humble response. *Equity & Excellence in Education, 50*(3), 331–332.

OUTRO

A Story about Black Laughter and
a Call for Spiritual Literacies

Meditation #8

There is so much joy and love in hearing Black laughter. The sounds are so distinct and like no other. Black laughter is contagious and unmatched. Black laughter is spiritual. Black laughter is life-giving and good for the soul.

Do you have any moments of Black laughter?

Brrnnnggg ... Brrrnngg—the bell rang for us to move into third period. As my second period students scurried out, my third block students trickled into the classroom. I quickly ran to the teachers' lounge to grab a snack. This particular morning, I was running late, and I didn't get a chance to eat breakfast. I needed a snack that would hold me over until lunch. I had to make a quick decision because I needed to get back to my classroom before the tardy bell rang. While I scanned the vending machine, a bright green and white bag of *Tom's Sour Cream & Onion* chips caught my attention. My mind went back-and-forth between the sour cream and onion chips or the *Tom's Barbecue* chips. Barbecue would be playing it safe because it doesn't disrespect your breath like the sour cream and onion chips do. Listen ... the sour cream and onion chips are good going down but the aftermath can be quite impactful. Everybody knows when you eat a bag of flavored chips, you need to have a piece of gum to the left of you. But it's a certain type of gum—neither Bazooka Bubble Gum nor Dubble Bubble Gum can save that breath. You need to have that Wrigley's Extra Long Lasting Peppermint Flavor, the Trident White Peppermint, or the Ice Breakers Ice Cubes types of chewing gum. Having the right type of breath refreshment as a teacher is important. Trust

DOI: 10.4324/9780429297052-11

me, you don't want to be melting students' pencils with your hot, sour cream and onion breath. But I digress.

After 30 seconds of contemplation, I stepped out on faith. Sour cream and onion it is! I did a quick happy dance because I was thankful to finally have nourishment. I returned back to my classroom. The students began to find their seats and slowly, the room became silent. A few minutes into the bell work, Taelore Jackson looked up and said, "Mr. J, your breath is going to be stank eatin' those sour cream and onion chips." Immediately, the silence broke from loud screams of laughter. The silly and goofy side of me wanted to join in on the laughter because it was funny, but the ego took over. I asked Taelore to remove herself from the class. After the students returned back to their bell work, I joined Taelore outside of the classroom to discuss her behavior. While speaking to Taelore, it took everything in me not to laugh out loud because the more I thought about it, she was absolutely right. As I stated before, you can't be eating those types of loud chips when you are required to have ongoing face-to-face conversations with people. After the conversation with Taelore, she went back inside the classroom, I remained outside for a few seconds. I couldn't hold my laughter any longer. This was such a Black moment. Taelore was schoolin' me on the literacy of breath. Just sayin' … breath is extremely serious in the Black community. Also, the Black students who laughed out loud at Taelore's comment also skooled me on the literacy of Black laughter. To illuminate, when the students laughed at Taelore's comment to me, I read their facial expressions and their high-pitched laughter. It was one of those moments when you know people are laughing at you and not with you.

Although I found this moment to be quite hilarious, it required me to go deep within. I reflected on how I have witnessed moments such as the one I had with Taelore between other teachers and students where other teachers would have given Taelore a referral wrapped in rhetoric such as *she was disrupting class during bell work*. However, as a result of Black girls' connection to the school-to-prison-nexus, my spirit knew I couldn't punish her. I continued to move deeper within—I discovered that it was my bruised ego and hurt feelings that had pushed me to remove her from the class. As a Black educator, I have my ego, but over time, I have developed a more alert and reflective mind and I've learned how not to work from a space of ego. It is important to note that there was a special literacy in me that knew the most I could do in that moment was to go out and have a conversation with Taelore. I knew taking it any further would be about my ego. I knew my decisions could have far more consequences for her because I understand what it means to inhabit a Black body in school spaces.

It's extremely serious, what could have happened if I did not go within. This moment taught me that I can mess up and make mistakes and that teaching requires us to do that deep soul and self work. As such, what I'm calling my spiritual literacies guided me in that moment. Spiritual literacies require that we not only know how to critically read the world but also critically read the soul and the self. I coined spiritual literacies in a book chapter I wrote in 2019. In the piece, I surmise that "spiritual literacies reflect and comprise one's spiritual wisdom, discernment, connectedness with the self and with others, resistance, and liberation within and beyond institutions and society-at-large" (Johnson et al., 2019, p. 215). Spiritual literacies are about being in a constant state of awareness and remaining at the seat-of-self. We cannot engage in racial justice work, if we are not whole. In short, I connect the *work* back to me and to who I am; I cannot engage in racial justice work without the spiritual. The following section is a reprint from my 2019 book chapter on spiritual literacies.

Spiritual Literacies

Spiritual literacies are revolutionary and divine and require what Johnson et al. (2019) call "critical race discernment" which is a racialized third-eye. Furthermore, the authors state that

> the third-eye is more of a spiritual phenomenon than natural one and is designed to help Black children not only read the word (e.g., be literate) but also *feel* and *read* their world (e.g., understanding how they are oppressed and the need to work against such oppression).
>
> *(p. 13)*

When embodying spiritual literacies, I argue that English educators, language and literacy scholars, and English language arts teachers should develop and possess critical race discernment. We have to possess this skill and practice to *feel*. Critical race discernment is the cornerstone of spiritual literacies. Spiritual literacies are a practice and embodiment that require the following components: rebirth, critical faith, critical spirituality, mindfulness, and self-care. See Figure 8.1.

Rebirth

Rebirth is the (re)awakening and renewal of a person who has undergone a spiritual death which has impacted them to begin a new life and journey as a spiritual being. Educators who are spiritual beings will experience numerous rebirths throughout our lives because we are continuously learning, reflecting, and growing deeper and more intimate with who our(selves) are on a *soul* level. A spiritual revolution is needed. Such an inclusion in English language arts classrooms can encourage English language arts teachers and youth to become more in tune with themselves on personal and spiritual levels. English language arts teachers and language and literacy scholars have the right tools at our disposal to create spaces where we provide contexts for youth to experience a rebirth.

Simply stated, when we introduce youth to racial justice pedagogies, theories, and curricula, it could potentially lead to their rebirth as well as our rebirth. The anti-Black racial violence that rests within schools demonstrates and communicates that there are people in these spaces who haven't gone through a rebirth and

Self-Care

Rebirth

Spiritual Literacies

Mindfulness

Critical Faith

Critical
Spirituality

FIGURE 8.1   Spiritual literacies components

who are not committed to racial justice. With this being said, a spiritual rebirth can revitalize our souls through focusing on purpose, the spiritual self(ves), community, and critical self-reflection. This notion of spiritual rebirth in the fields of English education and language and literacy studies would focus English language arts teachers' attention on teaching from the heart and soul while still providing youth with the tools to critically read the self and the world and excel academically.

Critical Faith

Critical faith is the belief and connection to a higher spiritual being. It is something we cannot see, but it's experienced through deep trust, connection, surrender, and manifestation (personal communication, Lumen, 2019). I believe critical faith is a personal commitment to justice and freedom; it's not merely about what you say but what you do (Cones, 2010). In previous sections in this book, I made reference to the radical imaginary. We cannot embrace and embody the radical imagination if we do not practice critical faith. By this I mean that our faith has to be attached to the social and political fight for justice and freedom. Critical faith is not anything new. My ancestors practiced critical faith. Historically, Black people have resisted dehumanization and oppression while assiduously fighting for our humanity through the practice of critical faith (Dillard, 2006). Our ancestors and elders knew that something new and different could be created but not without the praxis of exercising critical faith. Therefore, to (re)imagine English education and English language arts classrooms, we must begin to practice critical faith which is a commitment to the humanity of our children and youth. Cones (2010) writes, "the concretization of faith, actualized through love, can only be done by connecting faith with the praxis of justice" (p. 163). In short, we can't talk about having faith if we are continuously breathing life into whiteness and into the dehumanization of Black children and youth.

Critical Spirituality

Dantley (2010) centers critical spirituality within the field of educational leadership. Furthermore, he states that critical spirituality is rooted in the deconstruction of power structures, particularly as it relates to identity markers such as race, class, ability, language, sexual orientation, gender, religion, nationality, etc., and that the "spiritual" component is ever flowing, active, and intimate—it is connected to the self in hope for kinship with others, resistance, meaning, and the transformation of schools to become justice-oriented spaces. If secondary English teachers and English educators practice critical spirituality, it could possibly impact our beliefs, ideologies, and actions. Critical spirituality can move us to engage in a deep critical self-reflection process, and it propels us to create justice-oriented and humanizing curricula, pedagogies, and policies that create societal and political change (Dantley, 2010). I believe teaching is a spiritual calling (I'm talkin' to my justice-oriented and racial justice educators); critical spiritual English language arts teachers, English educators, and language and literacy scholars are not only committed to the language and literacy development and academic achievement of youth but also committed to connecting on a soul level with others and believe in the radical (re)construction of creating a better society than the one we currently live within.

Mindfulness

The mindfulness component of spiritual literacies is about being and feeling whole through the constant state of being aware of one's emotions, feelings, body, and energy. Through mindfulness, we (as educators) can begin to create spaces of joy and peace. I believe mindfulness is intentional and about remaining at the seat-of-self and at the seat-of-consciousness, even through the difficult and tumultuous times. Being mindful centers on emitting positive energy out into the universe—similarly, it is about changing your mindset and being more attentive to your thoughts.

Self-Care

Living in a world that is filled with racism, sexism, gender oppression, and violence, we have to practice self-care as a way to heal from the trauma and pain and as a way to take care of our physical, mental, and emotional health. Self-care makes us whole and it helps to improve the relationship we have with ourselves and with others. If educators aren't whole or don't take care of ourselves, we won't be able to fully support the well-being of Black children and youth. It is noteworthy to mention that self-care differs across people (Baker-Bell, 2017). For example, self-care can be prayer, meditation, writing poetry, exercising, surrounding oneself with people, making nutritious foods, etc. In certain communities and spaces, self-care is relegated to spa dates and pampering of oneself. Nonetheless, this creates a class-based imbalance that comes with self-care. People from working-class backgrounds might not be able to afford this type of self-care in the same way. In short, self-care is multifaceted and operates differently across different racial and ethnic backgrounds.

Although I have grounded my practices in the Black experience, I believe spiritual literacies can be taken up from educators who are from different racial, ethnic, and linguistic backgrounds. On one hand, many Black educators already come with certain spiritual practices based upon our racialized, gendered, and classed experiences. On the other hand, I know Black folks who are deeply religious but are not spiritually grounded. In addition, it is possible for white teachers to take up spiritual literacies. However, I don't think these practices will come naturally because there is an abundance of unlearning to undergo. We cannot teach spiritual literacies to youth in English language arts classrooms or in higher educational spaces if we haven't internally done the spiritual work to become whole as a person and as an educator through bringing the self into the classroom.

References

Baker-Bell, A. (2017). For Loretta: A Black woman literacy scholar's journey to prioritizing self-preservation and Black feminist-womanist storytelling. *Journal of Literacy Research, 49*(4), 1–18.

Cones, J. H. (1980/2010). The relationship of the Christian faith to political praxis. In C. Ellis & S. D. Smith (Eds.), *Say it loud: Great speeches on civil rights and African American identity*. New York: The New Press.

Dantley, M. E. (2010). Successful leadership in urban schools: Principals and critical spirituality, a new approach to reform. *The Journal of Negro Education, 79*(3), 214–219.

Dillard, C. B. (2006). *On spiritual strivings: Transforming an African American woman's life.* Albany, NY: State University of New York Press.

Johnson, L. L., Bryan, N., & Boutte, G. (2019). Show us the love: Revolutionary teaching in (un)critical times. *Urban Review, 51*(1), 46–64.

AFTERWORD

Fearlessness and Insurgency in the Building of Black Fugitive Futures

At the time of this writing, the world is experiencing what has been classified as a global health pandemic. As the novel coronavirus known as COVID-19 (or SARS-CoV-2) ravages communities across the world, many hospitals remain on the brink while their workers are placed in even greater precarity. While this should not be taken lightly, we must also be leery of the global pandemic of white supremacy. Never to discount the severity of the current moment, but we must also take into consideration what it means to live under a 500-plus year pandemic that large swaths of the population *still* refuse to acknowledge. Much of the misunderstanding lies in the unwillingness to recognize its reach beyond individualized acts of bigotry. While the use of racial epithets, burning a cross on someone's lawn, violently assaulting unarmed human rights protesters, or not interviewing a person because of the sound of their name are still problematic and triggering, we should understand these events as only a portion of the totality of white supremacy. Upon first glance, it appears to be the most visceral, but the systemic manifestations of racism/white supremacy remain ignored. When we take into account what racism/white supremacy is connected to (class, gender, age, (dis) ability, sexual orientation, etc.) and what it deeply impacts (educational, political, economic, and carceral systems), we are provided with an understanding of its structural function in the world. Mass incarceration, disinvested schools, housing discrimination, negation of voting rights, and lack of access to viable health care systems perpetually demonstrate the vestiges of white supremacy/racism in the daily lives of people throughout the world. *So what does this mean to those who say they are dedicated to educating Black youth?*

The book you've just read has dared to take us on a journey. In light of its gift to us, we should not betray it. Through a series of creative and tangible examples of what it means to work with Black youth, Dr. Johnson refuses to let us discard a simple question: *What does it mean for Black youth to navigate the hostility and anti-Black violence of the US schooling system?* Additionally, his series of meditations push educators to contemplate a question of fugitivity and the future: *What does it mean to work from a space of love knowing that "school" in its historical and contemporary function is never intended to do right by you?* More importantly, *what are you willing to do if you know this is true?* If we are clear that "schooling" is the arbitrary system of rewards for order and compliance to the state and "education" may include the disruption of said order because it continues to dehumanize you, then building the future looks very different. It will not come with a curriculum guide or a teacher's edition with answers in the back of the text. Instead, if you have made the decision to love Black children, *you have already made a decision to break the rules of the school and white supremacy.* If you dare to engage Black youth critically in a K–12 classroom, you have already conspired in an insurgent act. You have actively made a decision to revolt against the orthodoxy of word walls, scripted curriculum, high-stakes testing, and draconian discipline policies. You have made the decision to educate *in spite of* the school, not because of it. It is a fugitive decision. To engage in such acts, your love is required to be fearless and insurgent. In your decision to leave, the things that dehumanize you become unacceptable. You are no longer running from something, but you are running to something—something you have decided to create with others. Now you need to answer yourself in terms of what you are willing to do to build and protect it. *And this is just the beginning.*

If you choose to operate with these over-standings the road is not easy. It is not an understanding because it would be too easy to nod your head in agreement. It is an over-standing because you know it to be true and you are willing to do something about it. There is no magic pill that will grant you salvation. No potion exists that allows Black youth to see your revolutionary commitment. Because Black youth have earned the right to reject the systems that continuously marginalize and isolate them, their respect must be earned. They do not owe you a damn thing if you remain committed to the order and compliance of school. Lamar has dared us to leave. *Will you?*

David Stovall, PhD
Chicago, Illinois

INDEX

Note: Page numbers in *italic* refer to figures, page numbers in **bold** refer to tables and those followed by 'n' refer to notes.

abolitionist teaching 30–31
African American Language (AAL) 19
Alexander, M. 23, 26
Annamma, S. A. 116
anti-Blackness: conversations 3, 9; Critical Race English Education 6, 77; humanizing racial dialogue 5; instrumental roles 25; intersections of 59, 61; issues of 29; language and literacy education 30; literacies serve as rejection of 54; racial conversations 57; radical imagination 30
anti-Black racism 5; critical paradigms 19; Critical Race English Education 6, 51, 57–59, 130, 131; history of 2; MCTE's statement 38; physical violence 3; primary emphasis on 4; in schools 38–47; writing mirror practices of 78
anti-Black violence 8, 38–47, 55, 60, 112; multiple dimensions of 45; types of 41; in urban schools **42–43**
anti-racist curriculum 58
anti-transgender violence 2
Appeal to the Coloured Citizens of the World (Walker) 45
aside 87, 92–103, 123–124
at rise 87, 89

Baker-Bell, A. 44, 100, 113
Ball, A. 56

Baszile, D. T. 40
Bell, D. 101
BISOC (Black, Indigenous, Students of Color) 37
Black Arts Movement 55
Black ELA curriculum *see* ELA curriculum
#BlackExcellence 131
Black Freedom Movement 55, 57, 132
#BlackGirlMagic 131
Black joy 9, 31, 66, 132, 133
Black language 10n1
Black lives matter: Critical Race English Education 76; ELA classrooms 36; English education 36; in our classrooms/in school spaces 9, 16
#BlackLivesMatter movement 3–4, 8, 51; in ELA classrooms 36–38; in English education 36–38; language and literacy practices of 53
Black migrant students 29
Blackness 5, 8–9, 13, 39, 49–51; beauty of 21; classrooms spaces 129; complexity of 30, 61; criminality of 15, 24, 25, 27; Critical Race English Education 57–59; cultural memories 52; ELA classrooms 3, 4, 6, 9, 36–38, 85; fashion styles 113; justice-oriented partnership 52; pathological fear of 28; policing and

hyper-surveillance of 21; politics around
52; strength of 6
Black oppression 36
Black rage 129–130
Black women: age compression 28;
contributions of 55–57; critical race
autopsy 2; maltreatment of 2
Black youth 29; educational experiences of
40; marginalization of 40
Borsheim-Black, C. 45
Boutte, G. S. 5
Boylorn, R. M. 111
Bryan, N. 22, 28

Callier, D. M. 131
Chang, Y. 95
Civil Rights Movement 55, 57
Clinton (President) 25
Clinton, Hilary 27
colonization 24, 44, 91
Cones, J. H. 139
Context, Community, and Critical Race
Praxis in Education 67
Cook, D. A. 101
Cooper, B. C. 39
Crenshaw, K. 111
criminal act 40
criminalization 2, 25
critical English education, and literacy
studies 55–57
critical faith 138–139
critically responsive parent involvement
practices **94**
critical race autopsy 1–3
Critical Race English Education (CREE)
4, 7, 9, 57–59; family involvement 84–
85; reading/writing workshop 76–83
critical race theory (CRT) 1, 54–55, 98
critical spirituality 139
culturally unresponsive parent involvement
models **94**
curricular/pedagogical anti-Black
violence 41
curriculum 43, 45, 51–52, 71, *71*, 76;
anti-racist 58, Drug Abuse Resistance
Education (D.A.R.E.) 25; ELA 37,
56, 70, 72, 75, 95; grammar 79, *79*, 81;
literacy 58, 60, 61, 72; state-sanctioned
3, 8, 9, 52, 123; writing *78, 79*
Cutts, Q. M. 97

Dantley, M. E. 139
Davis, A. 30

Detention of Juvenile Justice (DJJ) 20
Doyle, J. L. 21
dramatic performances 8, 9, 88, 91, 102
Drug Abuse Resistance Education
(D.A.R.E.) curriculum 25
drugs 25–26; *see also* war on drugs derives
Dumas, M. J. 50, 55, 123

ELA classrooms *see* English language arts
(ELA) classrooms
ELA curriculum 37, 56, 70, 72, 75, 95
English language arts (ELA) classrooms
2–4, 6, 7, 9, 21, 31, 36, 39–41, 45, 46,
51, 52, 54, *87*; absence of race in 72–73;
anti-literacy laws 58; #BlackLivesMatter
in 36–38; language and literacy scholars
61; learning grammar rules 83; literacy
policies, and initiatives 59; narcissism
in 75; school leadership 59; white
ideologies and white supremacist
patriarchy 75; *see also* ELA curriculum
euro-American theories 6

Flint Water Crisis 37
forgiveness 15, 16
Freire, P. 57

Gordon, A. 100
grammar curriculum 79, *79*, 81
grammar lesson: centering standardized
English *80*, 80–82; on pronoun-
antecedent agreement 82–83
Groenke, S. L. 38, 57, 71

Hartman, S. V. 100
Hendrickson, Dr. 18–22
Hill, D. C. 131
Hill, M. L. 41
hooks, b. 129
Howard, T. C. 93

intellectual autobiographical writing 8
intermissions 106, 122–123

Jeffries, M. 55
Johnson, L. L. 99, 100, 137
Jones, S. P. 45
justice-oriented movements 55

Kelkar, K. 23
Kelley, R. D. G. 132, 133
King, L. J. 54
Kirkland, D. 57

Ladson-Billings, G. 28, 54
language and literacy policymakers 60–62
Lardner, T. 56
Letting Go of Literary Whiteness: Antiracist Literature Instruction for White Students (Borsheim-Black and Sarigianides) 45–46
Lewis Ellison, T. 123
LGBTQIA+ 29
LGBTQ movements 55
linguistic anti-Black violence 41
Linguistic Justice: Black Language, Literacy, Identity, and Pedagogy (Baker-Bell) 44
literacy curriculum 58, 60, 61, 72
Literature: The American Experience (Hall) 45
Lortie, D. 21
Love, B. L. 2, 25, 28, 31, 38, 41, 111, 132, 133
Lyiscott, J. 131

mass incarceration 8, 13; Black codes to 15; Black girls 28; of Black lives 23; Clinton's agenda 26; machine of 15
Matias, C. E. 5, 117
Maynard, R. 21, 29
Michigan Council of Teachers of English (MCTE) 37–40
mindfulness 139
monologue 4
Morrell, E. 56
Morrison, T. 39
Mosley, M. 112
Muhammad, G. E. 131

National Council of Teachers of English (NCTE), (journal) 4, 37
Nixon, Richard (President) 25–26

Obama, Barack 36
Oceguera, E. 23

Paris, D. 57, 90
Patton, M. Q. 96
performances 85–87; *see also* dramatic performances
Peterson, J. B. 24, 25
physical anti-Black violence 41
Playing in the Dark: Whiteness and the Literary Imagination (Morrison) 39
playwriting 87
PreK–14 education 4, 13, 21, 23, 36, 55, 60, 73, 93
PreK–22 students 21

prison industrial complex (PIC) 13, 14, 23–26
prison system 30
Pritchard, E. D. 113
professional development workshops 5

race, absence in ELA classrooms 72–73
racial storytelling 8, 86, 91, 99–101
racial violence: against Black lives 1; #BlackLivesMatter movement 3; critical race conversations 3; perpetuation of 38; racial storytelling 99; in school spaces 3
racial wounds 46
racism: critical race autopsy 2; Critical Race English Education 9; endemic nature of 1; issues of 45; *see also* anti-Black racism
radical imagination 4, 9, 30, 31, 69, 132–134, 138
radical love 130–132
Ragland, A. 36, 53
A Raisin in the Sun (Hansberry) 18, 19
Rankine, C. 39
reading and writing workshop model 18, 73; Critical Race English Education 76–81, 84–85; English education program 73; problems 73–76
Reagan, Ronald 25–26
rebirth 137–138
Reynolds, R. 93
Richardson, E. 36, 53
Rogers, R. 112
Ross, K. M. 50, 55

Sager, M. 23
Sarigianides, S. T. 45
#SayHerName 51, 53, 57
schools: abolition 30–31; anti-Black racism in 38–47; anti-Black violence in 38–47; black lives matter 9, 16; leaders and administrators 59–60; leadership, ELA classrooms 59; racial violence in 3; surveillance of black youth in 26–28
school-to-prison nexus 28–30
school-to-prison pipeline 22
Sealey-Ruiz, Y. 28, 57
A Seat at the Table, album (Knowles, S.)
self-care 139–140
Shipp, L. 131
Simon, D. 27
Smith, D. 90
Smitherman, G. 55, 56
Solórzano, D. G. 54, 102

spiritual literacies 136–140, *138*;
  mindfulness 139
state-sanctioned curriculum 3, 8, 9, 52, 123
state violence, modern-day 1
Stovall, D. O. 22, 30, 31, 67, 93, 132
Styslinger, M. E. 73
surveillance: of black youth in schools
  26–28; policing and hyper-surveillance
  of Blackness 21
symbolic anti-Black violence 41
systemic anti-Black violence 41

Tanner, S. J. 75, 99
Tate, W. F. 28, 54
traditional models, parental involvement 93
Trayvon Martin's death 38–47
Tuck, E. 91

United Negro College Funds 28
urban schools, anti-Black violence in
  42–43
US educational system 40

violence: American institutions by various
  types of 2; anti-transgender 2; linguistic
  anti-Black 41; modern-day state 1;
physical anti-Black 41; symbolic anti-
Black 41; systemic anti-Black 41; *see also*
racial violence

War on Dark People 26–27
war on drugs derives 8, 13, 25–27
white supremacy 1, 3, 5, 6, 9, 13, 21,
  24, 44; colorism reflects 119; Critical
  Race English Education 46, 57; critical
  race theory (CRT) 54–55; ELA
  Classrooms 36–38; justice-oriented
  movements 130; language and literacy
  practices 53; US public education
  system 129
Winfrey, O. 16
Winn, M. T. 91
Woods, J. 52
Woodson, C. G. 54
writing curriculum *78*, 79
Wun, C. 30

xenophobia 29

Yang, K. W. 91
Yosso, T. J. 54, 102
Young, V. A. 78

Printed in the United States
by Baker & Taylor Publisher Services